Team Leader Workbook

Sara Pope

*Illustrations by
Eileen Blyth*

Introduction

Getting Started

Meeting Management

Problem Solving

Conflict Resolution

Final Thoughts

Appendix

HRD Press, Inc. • Amherst • Massachusetts

Published by: HRD Press, Inc.
22 Amherst Road
Amherst, Massachusetts 01002
1-800-822-2801 (U.S. and Canada)
1-413-253-3488
1-413-253-3490 (fax)
http://www.hrdpress.com

ISBN: 978-1-59996-133-0

Editorial services by Sally Farnham
Production services by Anctil Virtual Office
Cover design by Eileen Klockars

Table of Contents

Chapter 3—Leading Your Team in Problem-Solving Efforts

Chapter 4—Dealing with Conflict and Problem Team Members

Chapter 5—Some Final Thoughts

Appendix

INTRODUCTION

Welcome to the exciting, challenging world of team leadership. You may have volunteered for the role; you may have been elected to the role; or you may even have been drafted into the role. Regardless of how you came to be a team leader, you are in for a leadership experience like no other.

Traditional Leadership

The picture many of us have of a traditional leader in an organization is of someone who decides what is to be done, how it is to be done, and who is going to do it. This traditional role also carries heavy responsibility—responsibility for initiating projects, responsibility for corrective action, responsibility for allocation of resources, and responsibility when things go wrong.

Team Leadership

The team leader role is very different from these traditional ideas. Successful teams are groups of people who work together toward a common goal with a sense of **shared** responsibility for meeting that goal. The greatest challenge in any organization using teams is gaining that sense of shared responsibility. Team leaders who have tried to use the traditional leadership style with their team have actually **decreased** the chances of team members developing the ownership and personal responsibility that is so necessary for success. Don't get me wrong! It's not only the team leader who falls into this trap, but also team members. We are all accustomed to the style we are familiar with—it's a style that works well in a top-down, autocratic organization. Supervisors and managers are in charge, and the "worker-bees" simply carry out the decisions of others.

We all recognize that there are numerous problems with this traditional style. A major one is that those who carry out the marching orders have no reason to ensure that they are doing it right and no sense of responsibility for the outcome. Although almost everyone complains about it, not everyone is ready to jump in and make decisions or take responsibility for outcomes. These are the people who may unknowingly push the team leader toward the "old" style leader. If you embrace and practice the skills, tools, and techniques taught throughout this workbook, you will be taking the steps necessary to guarantee that your style is the "new" style. It is a style that builds high performance, results-oriented work teams whose members hold themselves responsible for success **as a group.**

Are you ready to start working on the skills required to be an effective team leader? Let's roll up our sleeves and get started—if you've got a team to lead, you don't have any time to waste!

A Review of Critical Team Roles

Before we can really start talking about your role as team leader, we should define the terms we're going to use. In addition to the team leader role, there are several other critical team roles. Let's look at the definitions of these roles.

Role	Function
Sponsor	The sponsor is the person who is responsible for starting or chartering the team. The sponsor helps remove roadblocks, provides resources, and gives direction when needed. The sponsor is not a member of the team and only occasionally attends meetings. However, the sponsor does intervene if the team gets off track or is not productive.
Members	The members are part of the team because of their particular area of responsibility or expertise. Team members are responsible and accountable for the success of the team's efforts and thus must come to the team with a mind-set of working together toward a common goal, with a commitment to consensus, and with an attitude that the input of all members is critical.
Facilitator	The facilitator helps guide the team in using good team processes. The facilitator is a group-dynamics expert who ensures that the team is using the intellect, creativity, and input of all members through appropriate group processes and problem-solving techniques. The facilitator is not a member of the team.
Teams Coordinator	The teams coordinator monitors the development of teams in a facility. The coordinator's job is to make sure that projects are not being duplicated and that teams are working on issues that fit into the facility's priorities. The coordinator often acts as a facilitator when needed and coordinates the assignment of facilitators.

You may have these roles in your organization but call them by another name. That's OK. Just remember as you work through the book, these are the definitions that we will be using for each of these titles.

A Review of Types of Teams

As we go through the following chapters, we will also talk about leading three different types of teams—ad hoc teams, standing teams, and natural teams. Let's review those three definitions.

Ad Hoc Team

A group of people working together toward a specific, measurable goal or objective. It may consist of functional or cross-functional membership. Members usually serve on this type of team in addition to their regular job duties. This is a temporary team that always disbands once the goals have been reached.

Standing Team

A group of people who meet periodically to work on recurring or critical business issues. This team does not usually disband because of the long-term or recurring nature of the issue. Team membership is usually changed according to a set rotation schedule in order to keep the team fresh and involve as many people as possible. Members usually serve in addition to their normal job duties.

A group of people working on interrelated or interdependent tasks or working on common products. A natural team is an intact work group that may be functional (the accounting department) or cross-functional (a process team, work cell, or product team).

Each of these types of teams is formed for a different purpose. The purpose of the ad hoc team is to solve a particular problem or deal with a specific issue and then disband once the team goal has been met.

The standing team's purpose is to plan, strategize, and execute actions to deal with recurring or critical business issues. It is much broader in scope and is a long-term or permanent team.

The natural team is also a permanent team, formed for the purpose of accomplishing day-to-day work activities. A major purpose of this type of team is to incorporate continuous improvement, teamwork, and employee empowerment into daily work life.

Because each type of team is formed with a different purpose in mind, the challenges you will face as team leader will vary by the type of team. As you work through this book, you will see specific tips and techniques for leading the different types of teams. Regardless of which type of team you have been appointed to lead, there are some common elements to the job description. Let's look at a team leader's job description in detail.

Team Leader Job Description

Job Summary

The team leader is a team member and the administrative coordinator for the team. The leader manages team meeting time to ensure that the team is using good processes and drawing fully on the experience, knowledge, skill, and expertise of all team members. The team leader also ensures that team decisions are reached through consensus.

Principal Duties

1. Ensures that the team members understand the team goals/objectives and the team charter; works with team members to gain and ensure commitment to the team charter

2. Communicates with the sponsor if there is lack of understanding or arranges for the sponsor to meet with the team

3. Helps guide the team in developing and following a team plan; helps the team stay focused on the objective

4. Coordinates team meetings, ensuring that the agenda is prepared and posted

5. Helps the team manage meeting time and use good meeting processes, including meeting roles, process-improvement techniques, and problem-solving methods

6. Ensures that action plans and minutes are being taken and that minutes are distributed after the meeting

7. Ensures that team members are following up on action plans; helps identify and remove the roadblocks that prevent members from following through on assignments

8. Encourages and facilitates the involvement of all members; acts as a "cheerleader" when team members get discouraged

9. Leads the group (or encourages others to lead the group) in discussion, brainstorming, problem-solving efforts, or continuous improvement activities

10. Knows where to get help when the team needs it and oftentimes acts as the spokesperson for the team

11. Helps "sell" the team's recommendations to the sponsor, managers, supervisors, and other key personnel

12. Leads the team through conflict resolution methods and turns conflict situations into positive problem-solving efforts

13. Ensures that temporary teams are disbanded and results are publicized

Required Knowledge

1. Thorough knowledge and understanding of meeting-management techniques, group-process skills, consensus-building techniques, and group decision-making techniques

2. Knowledge of process-improvement tools and problem-solving methods and when to use them

3. Knowledge of the types and purposes of teams, team principles, and the elements of an effective team charter

4. Knowledge of where and how to garner resources and support for the team

Required Abilities and Personal Traits

1. Ability to communicate directly and assertively with all levels in the organization

2. Strong interpersonal skills; ability to get along with all types of people

3. Good listening skills

4. Acceptance by management and peers

Wow! Pretty hefty role, huh? Wait—don't panic. Take another look at the first line under job summary. The team leader, is simply a member of the team. As team leader, you share accountability for team success with all the other members of the team. Don't ever lose sight of the fact that you are in this with the other members of the team. You may play the point person, the contact person, the administrative coordinator, even the spokesperson—but when it comes down to success or failure, the entire team is in there together. Your greatest challenge is to carry out your role in a manner that continually keeps all members aware of that shared responsibility.

When you read all the duties on the job description, it's more than a little overwhelming. Let's break down the duties into manageable pieces and then develop checklists of activities to guide you through the job. There are five major headings that those duties can be categorized under:

Getting the Team Started	duties 1–3
Managing Meeting Time	duties 4–8
Leading the Team Through Problem-Solving Efforts	duties 9–11
Resolving Conflicts	duty 12
Closing out Temporary Teams or Rotating Leadership on Permanent Teams	duty 13

Having 5 areas versus 13 different duties is much easier to deal with. To keep things as easy as possible, we will focus the rest of the workbook on these 5 areas. Chapter 1 will outline the steps necessary for getting your team started on the right track. Chapter 2 will focus on your role in helping the team make the best use of meeting time. Chapter 3 will help you in leading problem-solving and continuous improvement efforts. Chapter 4 will cover your role in resolving and working through conflicts on the team. And finally, Chapter 5 will provide guidance for closing out ad hoc teams or rotating leadership on permanent teams. So let's get going!

CHAPTER 1

If you are the team leader of a newly formed team, there are certain activities that must be carried out to get the team off on the right foot. The following checklist outlines those critical activities:

Step-by-Step Checklist

✔	STEP
	Meet with the team sponsor to review and clarify the team charter.
	Meet with the team sponsor to help choose team members.
	Hold an initial meeting with the team to review the charter. Develop questions and coordinate a follow-up meeting with the sponsor.
	Determine team training needs. Coordinate with the team facilitator to schedule.
	Lead the team in developing team ground rules, operating guidelines, and other team planning activities.
	Ensure that the team develops appropriate measures of activities.

This checklist includes everything you need to do to get your team started. However, you might be feeling like there's something missing—how to do those things! We're going to devote the entire chapter to the "how-to's" for this checklist. We are going to take you step-by-step through the checklist and give you all the details you need to carry out each one of these steps successfully.

STEP 1

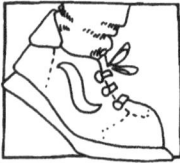

Meet with the Sponsor to Review and Clarify the Charter

Every team has a starting point. Whether ad hoc, standing, or natural, teams should be started with a written document that outlines the role, responsibilities, and expectations of the team. This document is called a charter and should contain the following information at a minimum:

Temporary Teams (Ad Hoc)

- The specific problem to be solved or goal to reach
- The time frame in which it must be completed
- The boundaries or empowerment limits
- The budget or other resources available

Permanent Teams (Standing and Natural)

- The mission or purpose of the team
- Boundaries or empowerment limits of the team
- The budget or other resources available
- Composition rules (who's on the team)

Since there are some differences in charters for the different types of teams, we're going to make it a little easier to see which type of team we are talking about as we go through this chapter and the rest of the book.

When reading this book, the symbols below will help you determine which type of team we are discussing:

A

Whenever you see this symbol, we're referring to an **ad hoc team.**

S

This symbol tells you that the discussion is about a **standing team.**

N

Look for this symbol to know that we're talking about **natural teams.**

What Do You Do if You Don't Understand the Charter?

If any of these elements are missing or confusing, talk to your sponsor about it. This is not the time to "wimp out." If you have concerns about the scope of the project, the time frame, or the empowerment limits, you must be direct and honest with the sponsor. Ask questions and get clarification. Many sponsors are new to the idea of writing charters and empowering team members, and they may have simply overlooked something in developing the charter. The only way the sponsors in your organization will get better at clarifying their expectations is to get feedback. Take the approach that you're both new to this and that you'll learn how to charter this team together.

What About Your Time?

If you are concerned about the amount of time that working with the team is likely to take up, talk with the sponsor about that. If the sponsor is your immediate supervisor, you may be able to talk through your other priorities and determine what can be put on a "back burner." If the sponsor is not your boss, you need to set up a meeting with the sponsor, your boss, and yourself to clarify where this project fits in to your other priorities. Remember, no matter how important this project is to you, if you just don't have the time, you can't do a good job.

What Else Should You Look For?

A Another problem to be on the lookout for with an ad hoc team is a charter that points to a specific cause or solution. Some problem statements include what the sponsor believes to be the cause of the problem. The team then works only on eliminating that cause, rather than ensuring that the root cause has been isolated. If your charter seems to include cause in the problem statement, ask your sponsor about it. Once you and the sponsor talk it through, he or she may want to revise the problem statement.

A sample of an ad hoc team charter for a group charged with reducing scrap can be found on page 1 of the Appendix.

In the sample ad hoc team charter, shown on page 1 of the Appendix, the goal statement tells the team members in very specific terms what they are to do: they are only looking at scrap on line #2. Being specific here helps the team know what the scope of the project is. The sponsor has not pointed to a particular cause—he or she left it to the team to determine causes. However, the sponsor did let the team know what would be considered a success—a 50 percent reduction in scrap. The team members will have to let the sponsor know how they plan to measure that success, but they know exactly what they are shooting for.

The charter also names the sponsor, the leader, the facilitator, and how long the project should last. Of course, the time frame is negotiable. If the team members don't believe the project can be completed within three months, they should discuss it with the sponsor. They may find that there are very good reasons for the short time frame and that they have to do some re-prioritizing of other issues. Or they may find that the sponsor is willing to stretch out the time frame somewhat. The key is to talk about it openly with the sponsor before beginning the project.

The boundaries let the members know what they can and cannot do. This team knows ahead of time that they have to live with product specifications as they are. They also know they can't move ahead with purchasing new equipment. On the other hand, they know they can get some bids and talk to the engineer about modifications if needed.

This particular team does not have an allotted budget, but can meet on overtime. The team also has assigned resources from the two areas that the sponsor thought might be able to help the most. This ensures that the team can get help from these support areas. The sponsor should meet with these resource people before assigning them to the team to help them understand where this project fits with other priorities.

This charter helps give the team a head start. However, no matter how much practice any sponsor has at writing charters, there will still be some questions from your team members. We'll talk specifically in Step 3 about how to get those questions answered.

A sample standing team charter is on page 2 of the Appendix.

Sunlike the ad hoc team's charter, the standing team's charter doesn't have a specific problem. Instead, it has an overall purpose for this team. As a matter of fact, it's a kind of "pie in the sky" purpose; this team will always strive toward this purpose, but never quite get there. That's exactly what we should expect to see in a standing team charter. To get some sense of accomplishment, a standing team will generate short-term goals that move the team toward that purpose. Just don't expect to see those short-term goals in your charter—as a team, you'll come up with those together.

Once again, the specific names of the sponsor and facilitator are listed. The team members are named as well, along with the team leader. With a standing team, membership may rotate over time. This keeps members from burning out, keeps fresh ideas coming, and ensures involvement from as many people as possible. The team leader role will probably rotate periodically as well. These are decisions the team will make over time.

The boundaries are also specified for the team. The team knows that policy cannot be changed without approval, that audits can be conducted, and that team members have the authority to ask for immediate changes in safety practices.

This team also has a little more in the way of resources than the sample short-term ad hoc team did. This team has a budget for the award program and will have to make some team decisions about how to administer that budget. The sponsor also tried to help the team by specifying who would provide them with clerical support.

Now take a look at the sample natural team charter on page 3 of the Appendix.

N This charter looks a little different, doesn't it? Like in the standing team charter, there is a team purpose—something the team will always be working toward. There's also a job description, letting the team members know what their responsibilities are. To really understand this charter, you have to remember what a natural team is. A natural team is an intact work group that works together day-to-day to accomplish assigned jobs. All we're really trying to do with a natural team is to get people to rely on one another and work together to accomplish tasks as efficiently and effectively as possible. A natural team can be organized around a product, a process, a customer, etc. A natural team can also be self-managed or can have an immediate supervisor.

The team's purpose is basically what brings us into work every day. Our sample charter tells this team that the main focus must be to produce widgets that meet or exceed quality standards. Other examples might be a training department that must develop and deliver training material. An accounting group might have a purpose statement as simple as "Perform all accounting duties for the organization."

The team job description gives us more details on the team responsibilities. Our sample lists maintaining machines, housekeeping, supplying internal customers, and covering each other's breaks.

The decision-making authority tells team members what they can take care of without approval or input from others. Generally, decision-making authority starts out fairly narrow with a new team and expands as the team matures.

The boundaries are also pretty straightforward in our example. The boundaries simply tell the team members ahead of time what they can't do. The decision-making authority tells the team the "cans" and the boundaries tell the team the "cannots."

An important thing to understand about a natural team is that, like a standing team, the purpose is long term—get the work done day in and day out. But the team also needs to look for ways to improve the processes and solve problems—in other words—not just get the work done, but get it done better. To do this, the team will have to set and strive for short-term, measurable goals—much like an ad hoc team. As a matter of fact, the team members will learn to sponsor their own ad hoc teams and then work, either as an entire team or in sub-teams, toward those goals they set for themselves. We'll spend more time on this concept when we discuss team measures.

Now it's time to put you to the test! You should have a good understanding of the type of thing to look for in a charter. We want to give you some practice looking at charters and identifying areas that might cause problems for you as the team leader or for your team members. Look at the cases below and on the next two pages and evaluate each charter.

Ad Hoc Team Charter

A

Problem Statement

Reduce customer service complaints about shipping delays by eliminating paperwork or streamlining the paper process.

Time Frame

3 months

Boundaries

Team can design new forms.
Team can eliminate forms.
Team cannot buy new equipment.
Team cannot make changes to shipping dock procedures without input from shipping supervisor.

Budget

Printing budget—$5,000

Resources

Steve Jones, Shipping Supervisor
Pam Smith, Facilitator

What problems do you see with this charter?

_____

_____

_____

_____

S

Team Purpose

The purpose of the plant safety team is to continually improve safety practices throughout the plant and increase employee awareness of safety issues.

Budget

$10,000 for safety award program

Resources

Facilitator as assigned by Teams Coordinator
2 members per year may attend company safety conference

Composition Rules

The team must always have at least two members from Production, one member from the Human Resources department, and one member from the Environmental department. The plant Safety Coordinator will not rotate off the team.

What problems do you see with this charter?

_____

_____

_____

_____

N

Team Purpose

The Customer Service team is to provide efficient, friendly, and immediate service to customers calling with questions regarding order status, product information, or problems.

Team Responsibilities

The team is responsible for timely and complete processing of all paperwork involved with customer orders; answering all incoming phone lines; providing break, lunch, and vacation coverage for team members; and identifying and eliminating problems that cause delays in order processing or shipment.

Boundaries/Empowerment Limits

At least two team members must be in the work area at all times.

The team may not meet more than one hour per week.

The team must notify the supervisor when an order is going to be delayed by more than 48 hours.

Team Sponsor:	Henry James
Team Facilitator:	Jeff Graves
Team Members:	Glen Jowers, Lisa Scott, Susan Tanner, Sidney Williams

What problems do you see with this charter?

_____

_____

_____

_____

See pages 4 and 5 of the Appendix to find the suggested answers for all three charters.

STEP 2

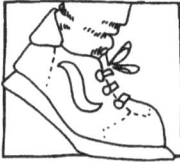

Meet with the Sponsor to Choose the Team Members

One of the first steps in setting up a new team is a meeting between the sponsor and the team leader. The sponsor has typically picked the team leader based on interest in solving the problem, skill, or expertise. The sponsor will often get input from the team leader on choosing the remaining team members. If you as team leader do have an opportunity to participate in choosing team members, you should keep the following factors in mind.

Each candidate should

- have some aptitude for solving the problem or interest in the issue;

- be motivated to solve the problem or address the issue;

- have some experience with the problem or issue;

- have the time available to serve on the team.

Notice that the only symbols on the list above are for ad hoc or standing teams. That's because with a natural team, you don't get any choices. The natural team consists of the intact work group—whether it's everyone in the department, everyone who works on the process, everyone in the area—the list of possibilities goes on. The make-up of the natural team is thus already determined. You simply have to work with the team members assigned. We'll talk later about the kinds of problems that can cause and some tips for dealing with it.

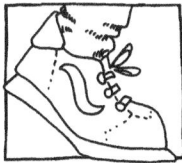

With standing and ad hoc teams, it's tempting to choose only teammates who think the same way you do or have the same views you do. However, the danger in this approach is falling into "groupthink." Remember, one of the major purposes of a team is to get a variety of perspectives. If everyone on the team has the same outlook, you don't need a team. Try to choose people who have different areas of expertise, who have different points of view, and who can look at the issue from as many different angles as possible. You should consider including customers and suppliers of the process on the team. They often have an entirely different perspective on the problem. You might even want to try to assemble people who haven't had an opportunity to work together in the past or who have disagreed on past projects. Conflict isn't all bad on a team, as you will see in a later chapter.

One more warning: Beware of team size. You may be able to think of all kinds of people who should be on this team. Just remember that the best team size is no less than 3 and no more than 10 members. Teams any larger than 10 members become very difficult to manage. Team meetings are harder to conduct, consensus is harder to reach, scheduling is like pulling teeth. So don't fall into the trap of picking everybody and their brother—keep the team size down!

STEP 3

Hold Initial Meeting with the Team to Review the Charter

This first meeting is critical. There are a couple of different ways you can carry out this important meeting. You (the team leader), the sponsor, and the team members can meet together to review the charter, ask questions, and clarify any misunderstandings. Or, the team members may meet alone or with the help of a facilitator to develop a list of questions or issues that they would like the sponsor to address. The sponsor then gets back to the team with answers or clarification. Some sponsors like this second method

because they have a chance to think through the questions and give the team definitive answers. Others are more comfortable with the face-to-face interaction with the entire team. This is a decision that you and the sponsor should make together.

Regardless of the approach, there are several things that you must do to ensure that your goal is met in this first meeting. In addition to coordinating schedules and ensuring that all members can attend this critical meeting, you must also do some preparation work. All members should receive a copy of the charter before the meeting. (And when we say before, we don't mean as they're walking in the door.) Get the charter out as much in advance as possible. One to two weeks is a good time frame. In addition, you must also develop an agenda for this meeting. But don't worry; it doesn't have to be an elaborate agenda. In addition to listing agenda items, you must also set estimated times for each agenda item. Inform members to bring their copy of the charter and a list of questions that they have about the charter, the project, or anything else about being on this team. An example of an agenda for an initial meeting is shown below.

MEETING DATE: July 27, 9:00 a.m.		**MEETING PLACE:** Conference Room A	
Purpose of Meeting: To review the team charter and develop questions			

Background Information:
    None
		Please Bring:
		    Your copy of the charter
		    Any questions you have	

AGENDA ITEM	**PERSON RESPONSIBLE**	**PROCESS**	**TIME**
Review the charter Form and answer questions	Bob Jones Sponsor	Open Discussion	20 min.
Discuss and develop any additional questions	Mary Ashford Team Leader	Open Discussion	20 min.
Set time and date for next meeting	Mary Ashford	Open Discussion	5 min.
NOTE: Bob will only be at the meeting for the first 20 minutes			

Let people know that this first meeting won't take more than 45 minutes. It might be a little shorter if the sponsor is not attending because all you will be doing is developing your list of questions. It may be a little longer if the sponsor plans to be there, answering the questions on the spot.

If possible, have a team facilitator at this first meeting. This meeting does not have a heavy agenda or even any decision making. But it is the first formal meeting, and you want to set the right tone. You may want to skip ahead to Chapter 2 and read some of the meeting-management techniques before you schedule this first meeting.

STEP 4

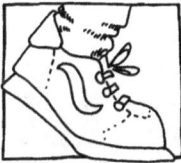

Determine the Team Training Needs

In your effort to put together a diverse group of people, particularly on ad hoc teams, you have probably assembled a group with very different levels of training or expertise in team activities. It is important to try to bring all members up to some minimum level of team skills before getting started on your team activities. There's more than one way to get this done. You might use a written survey such as the one in the Appendix on page 6. This survey could be handed out to members as they agree to serve on the team and brought to the charter meeting (in that case, be sure to mention it on the agenda).

If you would rather use a more informal approach to find out about training needs, you can simply conduct a straw poll at the meeting by asking for a show of hands to questions such as:

"How many have served on a formal team before?"
"How many have attended basic team training?"

Whichever approach you use, make sure you find out about experience with decision-making techniques, problem-solving tools, and meeting processes.

Once you know what people have already had in the way of team training, you should meet with the facilitator assigned to your team and determine just what you need for this particular team. All teams must have some basic team tools such as team roles for meeting management, brainstorming, and nominal group technique for decision making. However, some projects will need more advanced problem-solving or data-analysis techniques. Your facilitator should be able to help you in determining what you need to get started and at what point to add more advanced tools. We will talk about all these tools in Chapter 3.

STEP 5

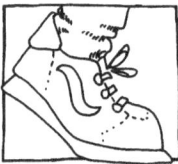

Lead the Team in Developing a Plan

Step 5 may vary somewhat depending on the type of team you are leading. If your team is a permanent team, you have more front-end work to do. If your team is an ad hoc team, you simply come up with some basics of how you'll operate and then get going. The following are some things you need for any type of team:

■ Ground rules
■ Meeting schedules
■ Role rotation

Let's look at these first.

What are Ground Rules?

All teams must have ground rules. The ground rules are the code of conduct that the team agrees to live by. An ad hoc team's ground rules generally focus on behaviors in the meeting setting since that's usually the only time that the team is together as a group. Most natural teams' ground rules include workplace behaviors in addition to the meeting etiquette. Some natural teams even have two sets of ground rules: one for meetings and one for day-to-day business. The team should make the decision as a group about what type of ground rules they need. Let's look at an example so that you have a better idea of what we're talking about.

Meeting Ground Rules
We will come to meetings prepared and on time. We will participate openly and actively. We will listen carefully without interruptions. We will stick to the subject.

How Do We Develop Ground Rules?

One method for developing ground rules is to brainstorm a list of the ways you do not want to behave in the meetings (or workplace). Once the team has that list, they can come up with a corresponding set of ground rules. The ground rules should be posted in the meeting room (or workplace) and should be read at the beginning of every meeting. The ground rules can be re-visited, edited, or added to as needed.

How Do We Set Meeting Schedules?

Other issues that any type of team must decide upon before starting are where, when, and how often to meet. One of the best ways to ensure that people are committed to attending meetings is to make sure they've had input into the frequency and times of meetings. It's probably impossible to come up with a schedule that is 100 percent convenient for everyone, but you may be able to come up with something that is less inconvenient.

One thing to take into consideration with an ad hoc team is the time frame allotted for the project. If you're facing a short time frame, the team may have to commit to more frequent meetings. Your job as the team leader is to participate fully in the discussion (as all team members should) and make sure that the discussion includes consideration of the time frame along with individual schedules.

Ad hoc team members may find it easier to accomplish their project if they set milestones. To do this, they must break down the project into phases and then set broad time frames for each phase. For example, a problem-solving team with a three-month limit came up with the following plan:

Phase	Activity	Completed by
Phase 1	Data gathering	January 22
Phase 2	Reviewing and analyzing data	February 5
Phase 3	Trials	February 26
Phase 4	Analyzing Results	March 15
Phase 5	Final decision Presentation preparation	March 30

This plan helped the team in two ways. The team did not feel as overwhelmed by the project they were charged with because members felt more confident that they could meet this timetable. The members also knew which phases would take the most time and effort and could plan their other work accordingly.

Some standing teams meet fairly infrequently. If the team is accomplishing their short-term goals through ad hoc or sub-teams, then the entire standing team may meet as infrequently as once a quarter. The frequency really depends on the team's purpose.

Natural teams usually meet frequently when they are first starting. They have a lot of decisions to make in terms of how they will operate, how they will meet their performance objectives, and how they will work together day-to-day. However, once they have this foundation in place, their formal meetings may become less frequent. They may have regular "huddle" meetings on the job, but they may have formal meetings only as they experience problems or take on major projects. However, some natural teams continue to have regular information-sharing meetings. Each team has to decide what will work for them, based on their responsibilities. (We'll go into great detail on all these types of meetings in Chapter 2!)

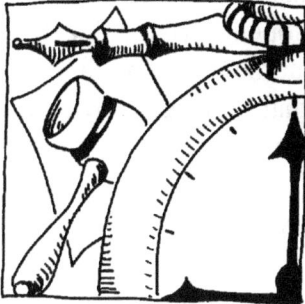

Successful teams use the following critical meeting roles in their meeting management techniques:

- Timekeeper
- Judge
- Recorder
- Gatekeeper
- Scribe
- Devil's advocate

We'll discuss the details of these roles in Chapter 2. But let's go on and talk about the early decisions the team has to make about these roles.

Role Rotation

To make the most of these roles, they should be rotated among team members. Sometime in the early life of the team, members must decide how frequently to rotate these roles and then develop a rotation roster. The team leader must ensure that the rotation schedule is followed. Many team members get comfortable in a particular role or in not having an assigned role at all. It's very important that everyone participate, and it's part of your job as team leader to make sure that happens. Get that expectation out on the table early in the life of the team.

Permanent teams (standing teams and natural teams) have a few additional issues to decide initially.

Standing teams must determine how often membership should rotate and develop procedures for educating new members. The decision on frequency will depend on the charge of the team, the frequency of meetings, and the amount of time and effort required on the part of team members. For example, if a team doesn't meet frequently and doesn't take up a lot of each member's time, members may feel that they can stay on the team for a year or more. However, if a team meets very frequently and eats up a lot of each member's time, you may not want members to commit to more than six months for fear of burnout. These are simply judgment calls. As the team leader, you must ensure that all members are participating in the discussion and that all views are being considered carefully.

Natural teams and standing teams should write a mission statement. The charter contained a statement of the team's purpose—what the team is to accomplish. However, a mission statement is a little different. It is developed by the team. It's a brief, easily understood statement of what the team does and how they do it. It gives the team something that they can rally around and feel ownership in. There is an example of a mission statement, as well as a worksheet your team can use to develop their statement, on pages 7 and 8 of the Appendix.

Because the natural team is a work group, they should also develop rotation schedules for tasks, schedule coverage, and do other day-to-day activities.

STEP 6

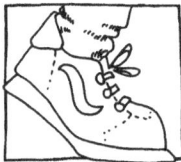

Ensure the Team Develops Appropriate Measures of Activities

All teams should be adding value to the business. It is difficult to know if we are truly doing that if there are no measures of success. Teams must determine how they are going to measure and report their success. Measures are something that really vary based on the type of team you are leading, therefore we're going to look at this topic by team types.

This measurement task is fairly easy for ad hoc teams because they have a specific problem to work on and usually have a specific number or percentage to shoot for. They simply have to develop a plan for reporting progress and documenting improvements. They can sometimes accomplish this by using a document called the measurement planning table. In addition to the example on the following page, you'll find this document in the Appendix on page 9, along with a blank form for your use on page 10.

When using this table, you simply decide what you're going to measure, how it will be measured, who is going to measure it, how long you will measure it, and what will be considered a successful solution.

Let's look back at the ad hoc team charter on page 1 of the Appendix. Let's assume that the sponsor and team leader revised the goal statement as "Reduce the number of customer complaints about shipping delays by 50 percent." The team filled out the measurement planning table as follows:

Measurement Planning Table	
What will be measured?	The number of customer complaints due to shipping delays
How will it be measured?	Phone complaints will be tallied by individual members Letters of complaint will be logged as they come in
Team member responsible for measurement:	Phone calls: individual team members Letters: team member responsible for mail for the week
How long will it be measured?	3 months
What will be considered a successful solution?	50 percent reduction

Ad hoc teams have a fairly easy job with this task because they are working on something that is very specific and very measurable. But what do permanent teams that have "pie in the sky" kinds of purposes do?

Standing teams also have to develop some kind of measures—otherwise, there's no way to know if the team's activities are worth the time and effort. Not only does the organization need an answer to that, so do the team members themselves. No one wants to waste time! We all want to feel like the things we work on pay off. Without that feedback, team members lose their momentum, and the team loses focus.

The standing team will actually have two types of measures. Let's look again at our sample standing team charter from page 2 of the Appendix. The safety standing team is charged with creating a work environment where people are not injured. It stands to reason that they will measure their overall effectiveness by looking at some type of safety record, maybe even several different measures. Monthly Reportable Accidents could be one measure. They may also look at visits to the nurse or activity reports that include non-reportable incidents. All of this information will measure overall effectiveness and should be determined early in the life of the team.

To actually make any progress toward the overall purpose, however, this team will have to identify some specific activities and projects to focus efforts on. Once these projects are identified, the team must then develop some short-term goals or objectives of those projects. There are several options for accomplishing those goals:

- The members may all participate in working as an ad hoc team toward the goal.
- The team may spin off sub-teams to act as ad hoc teams working on the goal.
- The team may sponsor an ad hoc team made up of team members from other areas of the organization.

Since the team will probably be working on more than one objective at a time, any combination of the above options may be used.

Once standing teams have determined how they are going to work toward the goal, they must decide how to measure accomplishment. Just like the ad hoc team, they may use the measurement planning table to measure it. Let's look at our safety standing team again. Monthly reports indicated that knife accidents were the cause of a large number of the reportable

incidents. The team decided to take several steps to reduce knife accidents. The measure of success was a reduction in knife accidents of 50 percent. Now this standing team has two measures—the overall measure of reportable incidents and the short-term measure of knife accidents.

Natural teams must also have measures. Like standing teams, they have two sorts of measures. Depending on what their responsibilities and duties are, they may have several performance measures. Just as individuals have a job to do, the team has a job to do and must keep track of how well that job is being done. A production team may have some of the following performance measures:

- **Number of widgets produced**
- **Number of rejected widgets**
- **Number of reworked widgets**
- **Amount of scrap produced**

These are simply measures of what the team is producing on a monthly, weekly, daily, or even hourly basis. The team tracks these performance measures in order to know if the job is getting done. These performance measures also tell the team where there are opportunities for process improvements or where problems may be occurring.

Once those opportunities for process improvements or problem solving arise, the team will develop some short-term objectives and goals and then come up with appropriate measures for those goals. And, just like the standing team, the natural team can work as an ad hoc team to accomplish the goal or use a subset of the team to work on the goal.

One way that natural teams are different from standing teams is that they don't have the authority to charter non-team members to work on projects. But really, if you think about it, that wouldn't make sense anyway. The natural team is supposed to be focused on the things that they themselves must do to get the job done—day-to-day work.

Summary

You have now made it through the start-up of your team. It is a lot of work, however, it's worth it. The more work you do on the front end, the smoother the team goes and the more likely it is to be successful. A successful team with all members feeling responsible for that success is your goal as a team leader. Starting your team with all the pre-work and effort that you've just been through is the way to set your team up for that success.

Now it's time to move on to the next major task—Chapter 2, Meeting Management.

CHAPTER 2

Y ou have gotten your team off to a good start by using the checklist of activities in Chapter 1. Now it's time to get your team rolling with good meeting management. Managing meeting time is one of the most critical skills for a team leader to master.

Why Are Meetings So Important Anyway?

Meetings are where the group gets a sense of being a team. It's also where the team makes the decisions that have to be followed up on. It's where the group decides what's important and what's not important. It's where members get their information, facts, and knowledge. Meetings help the members understand the team's goal and what each member must do to reach that goal. And, for some teams, the meetings are the only time the group is together as a team.

Three Types of Team Meetings

There are different types of meetings. The type of team you have and what you're trying to accomplish will determine which type of meeting you should be having. Let's take a quick look at the three different types.

Type of Meeting	Type of Team	Description	Purpose
1. Huddle	Natural	This is a brief informal meeting, lasting from 5 to 15 minutes. It usually takes place at the workstation and can be called at any time by any member.	The huddle meeting is used to share minor issues or problems that must be addressed immediately. It is also used to make daily work assignments or discuss the day's priorities.
2. Information Sharing	Natural, Standing, Ad hoc	This is a scheduled, formal meeting that is usually 15 to 30 minutes long. This meeting does have an agenda and uses the meeting roles and ground rules. The emphasis in this meeting is ensuring that all members have a chance to speak up and to ask questions.	The information-sharing meeting is used to report progress on action items and to update team members on numbers such as quality, production, etc. This type of meeting is used when the team doesn't have any decisions to be made or problems to be solved but needs to stay up-to-date on what is happening with current projects.
3. Problem Solving/ Decision Making	Natural, Standing, Ad hoc	This scheduled, formal meeting usually takes at least an hour or more. The emphasis with this type of meeting is on participation, interaction by all members, and consensus building.	Teams use these longer meetings to solve a problem they have previously agreed to work on. This type of meeting is also used to make decisions.

It is important that team leaders and members understand the difference between the three types of team meetings. Problem-solving/decision-making meetings require more time and more effort. Members may need to gather information beforehand and bring it to the meeting. This type of meeting may have to be broken into two or even three meetings if the team has limits on meeting time. On the other hand, the information-sharing meeting is fairly short and to the point. If members don't realize that this is the way it's supposed to be, they may feel that they should drag the meeting out to fill up the allotted meeting time. Wrong! Just recognize it for what it is—information sharing. However, if the only type of meetings you're having are information sharing, you need to sit up and take note. Take another look at your charter, talk to your sponsor, or get your facilitator involved. Remember, all teams should be doing something that adds value to the business, and this means analyzing problems and making decisions at least some of the time.

Each of the different types of meetings requires different techniques. The huddle obviously is the easiest; it's quick and to the point. The only real role that the team leader plays is to participate as any good member should and to make sure that everyone is included and that the team uses consensus if any decisions are made. The information-sharing and decision-making meetings take a little more effort. Since both of these are formal, scheduled meetings, there are certain activities that must take place. Let's look at a checklist of steps that a team leader must take before, during, and after team meetings.

Step-by-Step Checklist

✔	STEP
	Develop, publish, and circulate meeting agenda.
	Select the right location.
	Set up the room.
	Start meetings on time.
	Assign meeting roles.
	Use the parking lot form to stay focused.
	Ensure participation by using round robin.
	Enforce ground rules.
	Gain participation with questioning techniques.
	Get input by using brainstorming.
	Help the team develop a consensus mind-set.
	Guide the team in use of consensus-building tools.
	Follow up between meetings.

STEP 1

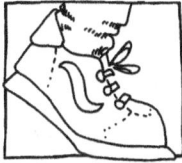

Develop, Publish, and Circulate Meeting Agenda

Agendas are one of the most important tools available to any team leader. Every formal meeting must have an agenda. The agenda is a list of meeting objectives, in priority order, that are to be covered during the team meeting. The agenda must be stated in terms of desired outcomes using action verbs (e.g., *decide, develop, recommend, resolve*) and should also include rough time limits for each agenda item. It takes some practice to write a good agenda. Obviously, the agenda should include some logistical information such as date, start time, and location. It's also a good idea to state a meeting purpose or outcome so that the group stays focused on the task at hand. An example of an outcome is "Complete the budget plan for next year."

If there is background information that members should read to prepare for the meeting or information they should bring with them to the meeting, use the agenda to remind everyone. The agenda should include the individual agenda items, person responsible, the process to be used, and the time allotted. Items should be as specific as possible and include an action verb.

On the next page, there is an agenda form. Using this form, develop the agenda for your first team meeting. Refer to the example on page 1-14 of Chapter 1 if needed. Once you have the agenda drafted, take it to the facilitator assigned to your team and get some suggestions. Don't worry about getting this first one perfect—this is something that you'll get plenty of hands-on practice with over time.

Exercise

Meeting Agenda

Meeting Date/Time _____ Location _____

Purpose of the Meeting:

Background Information:

Please Bring:

Agenda Item	Person Responsible	Process	Time

Agenda Writing Tips

Don't underestimate your times

Don't get too ambitious in setting the agenda. It's better to have too much time allotted than to try to rush through important issues. It also leaves team members feeling lousy if they can't get through the agenda. It may take some time to develop skill in estimating times, and there are some things that are just going to take more time than you thought.

Set the agenda early

Once you have drafted an agenda, it should go out to the members about a week in advance. If you send it out more than a week ahead of time, people may forget about it or misplace it. Less than a week doesn't give members much time to think through the issues.

Use team meeting time to plan next meeting

If a team meets weekly, it's a good idea to use the last five minutes of one week's meeting to draft the agenda for the following week's meeting. That draft agenda should be posted somewhere accessible to all members so that it can be added to or revised as the week progresses. When using this approach, the team leader should make sure that a final agenda is published at least a day before the meeting.

Get agreement to stick to the agenda

Make sure that you review the agenda at the beginning of the meeting. Ask if the group agrees with the agenda and get commitment at the beginning of the meeting that this is what the team should focus on.

STEP 2

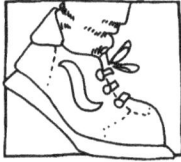

Select the Right Location for the Meeting

Let's talk about the meeting room itself. This shouldn't matter, right? Once you've got your agenda, you can meet in just about any setting and have a good meeting, right? Wrong! Where you meet can affect the group. Just having a good room will not ensure a good meeting, but a bad room can certainly make it tough to have a good meeting. When you can't hear one another, when you have a lot of distractions, when you can't see well, or when the room is hot and stuffy, you will have a hard time concentrating on the content of the meeting, no matter how well organized the meeting is.

When choosing a room, there are a couple of things to keep in mind. If the room is too big, the group will feel lost and overwhelmed. If the room is too small, the group will feel crowded and maybe even claustrophobic. Try to reserve a room that is the right size for the group. If you have to choose between a room that's too big or too small, go with the one that's too big. You can always set up your table and chairs so that you make the space seem smaller. When a room is too small, there's little you can do about the stuffy, cramped feeling it creates. If possible, try to meet in the same place for every meeting. You will eliminate problems with people wandering around looking for the right room, you can keep your ground rules posted, and you won't have to do as much rearranging.

STEP 3

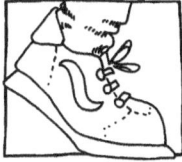

Set up the Room

Believe it or not, how you arrange the meeting room is important. The arrangement of tables and chairs can do a lot to encourage participation. It can also do a lot to leave people out. One of the best ways to arrange a meeting room is in a semicircle with the group looking toward a flip chart or presentation screen. With this setup, team members can all see each other and can focus on the task at hand. If the team will not be using a flip chart, the other option is to have the group in a circle. **Don't** set up the room in a way that encourages or allows participants to sit away from the rest of the group. Sometimes meeting rooms have extra chairs around the perimeter, encouraging shy or less participatory members to sit outside the rest of the group. If your meeting room is like that, stack the extra chairs out of the way or move them out altogether. Also make sure that you have enough chairs around the table for the number of people you are expecting.

STEP 4

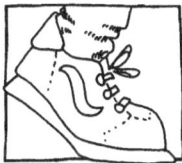

Start Meetings on Time

We've said that the meeting start time should be specified on the agenda. That start time should not just be a suggestion—members should think of that as set in stone. Start your meetings on time and end them on time. This courtesy will go a long way toward creating positive feelings in the team members about being a part of this team.

STEP 5

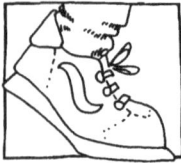

Assign Meeting Roles

One way to keep members very involved in the meeting process itself is through the use of team roles. As the team leader, you want to instill in all team members a sense of responsibility for good, productive meetings. If you are constantly keeping up with all aspects of the meeting processes, the team will always see the responsibility for the meeting as falling on you. So, since we have already said that one of the most important things you do as team leader is to get all members to feel responsible for the success of the team, it stands to reason that you've got to establish that shared accountability for meetings as well. The best way to do that is to use the following meeting roles.

Timekeeper

This is the team member who ensures that time constraints are observed during the meeting. The timekeeper issues friendly reminders when discussions on a topic must come to an end.

Gatekeeper

This team member has the role of keeping the team on the subject at hand. This person "keeps the gate" on the agenda and limits discussion to the topic.

Recorder

This team member writes on the flip chart as needed during the meeting. The recorder must listen carefully and capture the meaning of the idea without editorializing.

Judge

This member enforces team ground rules in a friendly manner, using the technique agreed upon by the team.

Devil's Advocate

This member agrees to point out the flaws or possible objections to all the options that the group is considering. This role helps the group consider opposing sides of every issue.

Scribe/Notekeeper

This team member keeps track of decisions that are made or actions to be taken by the team. The scribe usually fills out an action minutes form and distributes it to team members (and possibly the sponsor) after the meeting.

One point: not all teams use all the roles. Some teams combine some of the functions, particularly if they have just a few members. However, remember your goal is involvement by all, so try to make sure everyone has some type of role in the meeting. It's also a good idea to rotate these roles. Everyone should know what it's like to carry out each role.

Assignment

There is a form for assigning roles on page 11 of the Appendix. Use this form at your next meeting to determine role assignments.

STEP 6

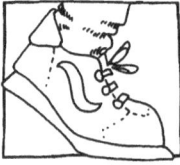

Use the Parking Lot Form to Stay Focused on the Agenda

Once the meeting starts, the gatekeeper can use a parking lot form to keep the group focused on the agenda. When topics are brought up that are not on the agenda, it is "parked" on the parking lot form. Using this tool ensures that the team can stick to the agenda without forgetting about the issue. The team either addresses the parking lot issue at the end of the meeting, puts it on the agenda for the next meeting, or assigns it to someone as an action item to follow up on. This approach shows respect for the views of the person bringing up the issue, keeps important issues from falling through the cracks, and keeps the group on task. The parking lot form is usually kept by the gatekeeper. There is a sample parking lot form on page 12 of the Appendix.

STEP 7

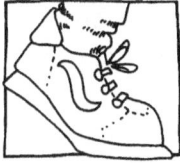

Ensure Participation by Using Round Robin

Round robin is one of the simplest tools you can use to keep everyone involved in a discussion. Round robin simply means that members take turns speaking. There are no interruptions unless someone has a question or point of clarification. The discussion usually goes around the table in sequence, thus the name *round robin*. This is one of those little tricks we learn in kindergarten and then forget how valuable it can be throughout life. The interesting thing about round robin is that it addresses participants at both extremes—it encourages and brings out quiet members by ensuring they have opportunity, and it forces dominant, talkative members to allow others a chance to speak.

STEP 8

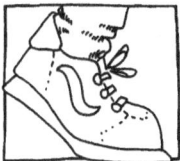

Enforce Ground Rules

Ground rules are critical to any type of team. The ground rules are a code of conduct that the team agrees to follow. They usually consist of 10 or fewer statements of expected team behavior. Ground rules are developed by consensus in the early stages of a team's development and may be altered from time to time. Ground rules are often posted where all can see and are often read at the beginning of each meeting to remind all members of expected behavior. Of course, you already have your team's ground rules since you followed the checklist for getting the team started. However, remember that you can revisit them at any time to add, edit, or revise. Just looking at the ground rules every once in a while is a good way to keep the team focused on following them. The team should also appoint a judge to enforce the ground rules—you must remember seeing this role in Step 5! The team has to decide on a technique for the judge to use. Some teams simply use a verbal reminder, others use a bell or whistle, while some even assess a penalty! If you use a penalty, keep it light—a dime, a quarter, having to bring coffee for everyone to the next meeting, etc. The team should decide on a technique in the initial team meeting.

STEP 9

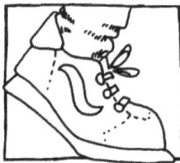

Gain Participation with Questioning Techniques

Sometimes in all the planning and working with teams, we forget about the elementary, common-sense things we can do. Asking specific questions of individual team members is one of those elementary actions that gets them involved in the meeting. Starting a round robin by calling on an individual by name with a clear, concise question will get the conversational ball rolling much faster than simply throwing out a question to the team in general. Using open-ended questions is another technique the team leader can call into play. Open-ended questions are questions that can't be answered with yes or no. Open-ended questions encourage the speaker to elaborate on their response. An example of an open-ended question is:

Ed, how did you deal with that problem when it happened to you last week?

This kind of question is more likely to get a response than:

Ed, do you have any ideas on how to deal with the problem?

Some open-ended questions aren't even questions—for example:

Ed, describe what you did when you had this problem last week.

Ed, tell us what happened when you . . .

Asking these specific, open-ended questions and directing them to individual team members is guaranteed to give team discussions a boost!

Additional Questioning Tips

TIP #1   Allow time for the speaker to respond after asking a question. The person may need to think through a response.

TIP #2   Ask only one question at a time.

TIP #3   Use closed-ended questions to gain commitment to an action or to close out a discussion.

TIP #4   Don't always call on the same person first. Other team members might think that you value that person's opinion more than others'.

TIP #5   If you call on a team member who doesn't seem to be able to respond, move on to another member. You might say something like, "Jim, let me give you a chance to think about that for a minute. Leigh, what do you think?" But make sure that you go back to that first member to give him or her a chance to respond.

STEP 10

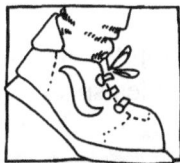

Get Input by Using Brainstorming

Brainstorming is an important participation technique. This is simply a method of generating alternative ideas. Following the rules of brainstorming will encourage involvement by setting up a process that promotes creativity and input while protecting members from ridicule or embarrassment. The purpose of brainstorming is to generate as many ideas as possible. Remembering that purpose will go a long way in helping you carry out the process correctly. It's not to come up with the best idea, it's not to discuss and evaluate ideas; it is simply to generate those ideas. The other steps—evaluating and choosing—come later.

Here's how it's done. Each member of the group states their ideas, and a recorder writes the ideas on a flip chart. There are, however, a few rules:

- No criticism, evaluation, judging, or even discussion of ideas is allowed during the brainstorming phase.
- The more ideas, the better—nothing is too crazy.
- The recorder may not editorialize, rephrase, or change the wording.
- The recorder may ask for clarification if needed to capture the idea.

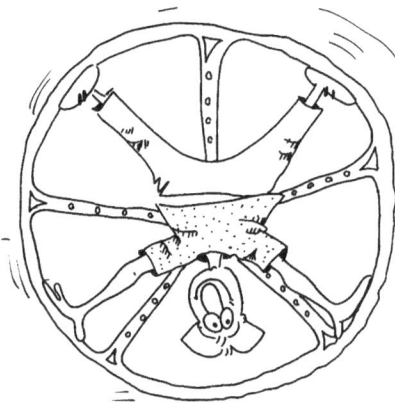

As simple as this technique is, it is one of the most powerful tools available to your team. Once members understand that no criticism is allowed and that ideas won't be changed or manipulated without their input, the involvement level skyrockets! You may have to play traffic cop at first. People are used to discussing and evaluating ideas as they come up. You or the facilitator will have to do a lot of reminding of the rules at first, but after a while, it will become second nature.

There are two different ways you can conduct a brainstorming session:

Freewheeling

When using this method, team members simply call out ideas. There is no particular order; whoever has an idea speaks out.

Structured

With this method, team members give ideas using a round-robin format. Team members speak only when it is their turn, and anyone who does not have an idea can "pass." The process is not complete until all members pass.

There are advantages and disadvantages to both methods. Freewheeling generates a lot of ideas in a short period of time. It can be very exciting and spontaneous. Members just shout out ideas as they occur to them. Often, one member's idea will spark an idea for another. As a matter of fact, it goes so quickly that you may want to use two recorders, each capturing every other idea, to avoid overwhelming the recorder. The downside to freewheeling is that quiet members may not get a chance to participate—it's easy for your dominant members to take over.

The structured approach helps protect everyone's right for input. It encourages quiet members while de-emphasizing dominant members. However, it's not quite as spontaneous and doesn't generate the same excitement that freewheeling does. The structured method doesn't allow for just blurting out ideas; if one idea sparks another, members still have to wait their turn. Unfortunately a good idea may be forgotten before the next turn rolls around. There is a trade-off, however—you gain the input of all, but you lose some of the spontaneity.

Whichever approach your team decides on, don't forget the rules of brainstorming. These rules apply regardless of the approach.

Additional Brainstorming Tips

TIP #1

When using structured brainstorming, keep a pad in front of you for writing down ideas. Then if someone else's idea sparks one for you, you won't forget it.

TIP #2

Compromise between the two options. Start with structured and when members begin to pass, go to freewheeling.

STEP 11

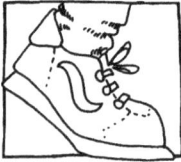

Help the Team Develop a Consensus Mind-Set

Obviously, your team will take action and make decisions during these well-organized meetings. There may be times when it is a real challenge to get this diverse group of people with different ideas to come to some kind of agreement.

A couple of things that you have to remember about team decision making is that for most members, consensus is a new concept. Our culture and society have tended to use majority rule (voting) for decision making. The problem with voting in teams is that it results in winners and losers—and the losers tend to do little to help ensure the success of the decision, if not actively work against it. Once again, you have to remember that shared accountability. You probably won't get a sense of accountability from the dissenting voters. Consensus decision making is the only way you'll get that accountability. It definitely takes more time, and it definitely takes more energy. However, the payoff is worth it. A team working toward an outcome that was decided upon through consensus has a totally different attitude, spirit, and energy than a group that has been forced to give in or go along with the majority.

Before we go any farther, let's define consensus:

> Consensus is group commitment to a decision. When consensus is achieved within a team, each member is willing to support the decision and do his or her part to ensure a successful outcome.

All the tools and techniques we have covered so far will help in building consensus. Consensus is not something that simply occurs at a single point; it's something that the group builds toward and works on over a period of time. They accomplish it by considering every team member a critical part of the group, by listening to the views of all members very carefully and considerately, and by presenting their own views clearly and concisely. By developing a meeting environment that is well organized, involves everyone, and protects everyone's right for input, you have helped create a setting that promotes consensus. As the team leader, you must also help the team focus on finding the right answer in terms of the team's goal, rather than deciding who is right. We will talk more about that in Chapter 3, Leading Your Team in Problem-Solving Efforts.

Helping the team reach consensus is time consuming and some-times difficult. Your major responsibilities are to make sure all members have an opportunity to speak out and to hear what others think, to keep the group focused on the decision to be made, and to suggest methods or procedures that the group can use. In the next step, we will cover some tools that can help your group reach consensus decisions.

STEP 12

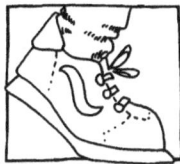

Guide the Team in the Use of Consensus-Building Tools

Remember, consensus is not something that occurs in a single point in time—the team builds toward consensus by using all the involvement techniques we've covered so far. However, there are some tools and techniques that will help you in guiding the team to consensus decision making.

Nominal group technique (NGT) is one technique for reaching consensus. It can be very helpful in building consensus for any decision that has several options. To use NGT, you must follow the phases outlined on the following pages.

Phase 1: Generate Ideas

All team members write down their ideas or preferences on the issue or topic. This is done individually. Whenever possible, let team members know in advance of the meeting so that they can bring their written ideas to the meeting. If that's not possible, then make sure they have plenty of time to develop their individual lists in the meeting.

Phase 2: Record Ideas

Team members offer their ideas in a round-robin format, and the recorder writes all the ideas on a flip chart. There is no editorializing or commenting allowed during this phase.

Phase 3: Discuss Ideas

The group goes back through all the ideas, discussing each one thoroughly to ensure complete understanding. Team members may ask clarifying questions but cannot discount or put down any ideas. If there are ideas that are similar but simply worded differently, they may be combined in Phase 3, as long as the contributing parties agree.

Each team member individually "scores" the ideas. The recorder documents and adds up the individual scores to determine the team's preference. There are a number of ways the team can rank order the ideas. Rank ordering, 10-4, and weighted voting are all options that can be used in the individual scoring.

Rank Ordering

If there are 10 ideas, the top preference receives 10 points; next, 9 points; and so forth. If group members wish to reduce to a smaller number, they determine the number they wish to reduce the list to and assign that number to the top choice (e.g., if the team wants a final list of 5, the top priority receives 5 points; second priority, 4 points; third priority, 3 points; fourth priority, 2 points; fifth priority, 1 point).

Whenever possible, the team should agree on the criteria that each member is to consider in their individual ranking. For example, if the team decides that cost is the most important factor in this decision, then each member chooses their favorite option that meets the low-cost criteria. Other options for criteria are importance, cost, control, difficulty, time, resources, impact on quality, impact on customer, etc.

Sometimes this technique is a little confusing until you see it in action, so let's take a look at an example of a group using this technique:

The safety team at the AJAX Company noticed that there was a higher rate of accidents in one particular area of the plant. This rate had been steadily climbing for six months. Each individual team member brought a list of possible causes to the meeting.

(Phase 1). They went round robin and the recorder captured the following list **(Phase 2)**.

- ✓ Untrained personnel
- ✓ Poor lighting in the area
- ✓ A lot of new employees working in the area
- ✓ Uneven floor in the area
- ✓ A lot of foot traffic in the area
- ✓ Employees in the department are simply careless
- ✓ No safety reminder signs in the area
- ✓ Forklifts moving in and out of the area

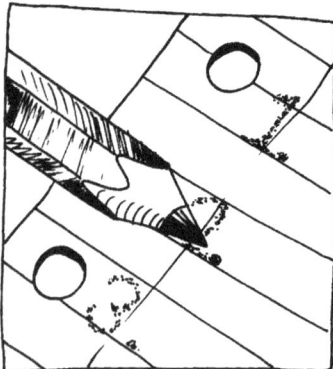

After the group had exhausted all ideas, they went through the list and discussed all these possibilities **(Phase 3)**. The member who contributed untrained personnel to the list said he was thinking about the fact that there were so many new people in that area. The group combined untrained personnel and new employees, leaving seven possible causes.

The team decided to narrow this list down to the three most likely causes, so each member took a few minutes to think about the choices. Once all members had written their three choices down on a piece of paper, the recorder captured all the scores and added them up as follows **(Phase 4)**.

1. Poor lighting in the area   3332
2. A lot of new employees working in the area / untrained personnel   22 11
3. Uneven floor in area
4. A lot of foot traffic in the area   3
5. Employees in the department are simply careless
6. There are no safety reminder signs in area   2 11
7. There are a lot of forklifts moving in and out of the area

The group discussed the outcome **(Phase 5)**, and the member who had assigned a 3 (the highest priority) on number four agreed with the others that there had always been a lot of traffic in that area without this problem and agreed that the team should address items one, two, and six. The team leader went round robin to ensure that everyone could agree that the team's top priorities for action were items one, two, and six. All team members agreed.

One member agreed to talk to the maintenance supervisor about the lighting and new signs **(Phase 6)**. Another member agreed to schedule and conduct safety training for all new employees in the area within two weeks.

This is an example of the technique in action. With this particular example, there was not much in the way of criteria for the team to use. However, whenever possible, the team should determine some kind of criteria for choosing options.

Admittedly, it is a little difficult to use NGT the first time or two that a team tries it. However, it's one of those things that if you hang in there, it will become second nature. One team leader says that she became a believer when she found herself using it at home to settle a disagreement on where the family was going on vacation—and it worked!

PIN

PIN is another discussion technique that may help in reaching consensus. When using PIN, team members must state something positive (P), something interesting (I), and then something negative (N) about the idea, proposal, or issue that the team is discussing. PIN helps the team look at all aspects of an idea before trying to reach a decision about it.

10-4

The 10-4 technique is similar to NGT. With the 10-4 technique, participants generate a list of alternatives to choose from. Once that list is generated, individuals rank their preferences by allotting points. Each member has a total of 10 points to "buy" their favorite alternatives. The only limits are that no more than 4 points can be spent on a single item and no more than 4 items can be bought. This technique works very well when there are more than 5 but less than 15 options to choose from.

Weighted Voting

Weighted voting is another technique available for choosing from several options. The technique gives the team information about the strength of individual preferences and helps to surface the opposing viewpoints. To use weighted voting, the recorder sets up a grid like the one on the next page.

Each member receives a set number of votes to distribute. The number of votes is determined by multiplying the number of options by 1.5. The team determines criteria for choosing options—cost, difficulty, control, etc. Each member then individually decides how to distribute the points. After allowing enough time for members to carefully consider and write down their votes, the numbers are recorded in the grid. The recorder totals the individual preferences to see which are the team's preferred options. Once the team has identified those preferred options, they can focus the remainder of the discussion on those.

The example shows a team of five people who were considering eight options. Each team member was given 12 points to allocate (8×1.5). The options have been given letters for ease of recording.

	A	B	C	D	E	F	G	H
Rebecca	2	3	3	1	1	0	0	2
Susan	3	5	0	0	0	2	1	1
Mark	2	2	1	1	2	2	2	0
John	4	0	0	0	4	2	1	1
Bill	3	3	3	0	0	2	1	0
Total	14	13	7	2	7	8	5	4

The totals on the grid indicate that the team prefers options A and B. This weighted voting exercise should help this team narrow the focus of their discussion to those two options.

Some Additional Consensus-Building Tips

TIP #1

Find the points that the group can agree on before focusing on the areas of disagreement—build on those successes.

TIP #2

If most of the team seems to prefer one alternative, ask for ideas on revisions to the option that make it more acceptable to the dissenting members.

TIP #3

If the team is stuck between two options, propose "trial periods" for each option.

TIP #4

Explore the idea of choosing more than one alternative. We tend to think in terms of one right answer when actually some of the options are not mutually exclusive.

TIP #5

Let the group "sleep on it." Sometimes delaying the decision can give people an opportunity to come up with new or creative approaches.

Look into the future—look at each alternative and predict the best and worst possible outcomes of each.

Try role reversal—if two people are disagreeing, ask each to summarize the other's point of view. Sometimes this clears up miscommunications or misunderstanding and stimulates new ways of looking at the alternative.

If you are a leader of a team that can't come to a decision, it might simply be because the team just has not hit on the right answer yet. You may have to delay resolution until the team can gather more information. At this point, as the team leader, you should get input from the team sponsor about deadlines for final decision and options for management intervention if the team can't reach final consensus. Also, don't forget throughout this entire process to rely on an outside facilitator. This neutral, unbiased outsider can be a great help in taking some of the emotion or tension out of the situation.

STEP 13

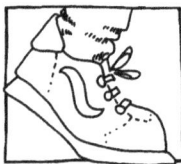

Follow up Between Meetings

You have spent a lot of time making sure that your team's time is not wasted—both in planning and in the conduct of the meeting. So—we are now absolutely certain that this team is going to be successful—right? Well . . . not yet. Even if you have a great meeting and make a solid decision that everyone supports, there's still one detail to take care of—implementation.

One way to help ensure that team decisions are followed up on is to write the decisions down. Committing the decision to paper helps commit people to action. An action minutes form or action steps form is something that many teams have found helpful. This simple form has a space to write the decision made or action taken in the meeting. It also includes who took responsibility for the action, any resources needed to carry it out, and the date by which it will be complete. This form specifies the who, what, when, and where that will turn talk into action. There is an example of a completed action form on page 13 of the Appendix.

In addition to completing the form, you can do a couple of other things to help members follow through on actions. Always review the action form at the beginning of each meeting to get an update on how members are progressing with individual action items. If a team member is having trouble carrying out an assignment, find out what is causing the delay. You may need to renegotiate the time frame or garner more resources. The team may be able to find a way to break the assignment down into two or more parts so that several members could be involved. By lessening the responsibility on one person, you increase the likelihood of success. The most important thing is to keep the team focused on the decision or action until it becomes a reality. Don't let it fall through the cracks— the action form is the best way to keep up with it. Each time you review the form, carry the unfinished items over to the next week's form. The item stays on the form until the status column says COMPLETED.

TIP #1

If there are long periods of time between meetings, follow up with the team members between meetings on the status of assignments.

TIP #2

If a team member seems to be having trouble carrying out the assignment, ask if he/she needs additional resources. Ask for specifics on how you can help. Communicate a willingness to go to the sponsor to garner additional resources if needed. Note: Do NOT maim, blame, or shame! Assume the person means to get it done, but has simply run into roadblocks.

TIP #3

Rotate responsibility for action items as much as possible. Review past action forms to ensure that the same team members are not always ending up with assignments.

TIP #4

Take your share of assignments but make sure you're not taking more than your fair share. Occasionally the team will "dump" as much as they can on the team leader.

We've covered a lot of techniques throughout this chapter. Most of these techniques are designed to organize and manage your meetings, while keeping people involved and participating. Now we're going to put you to the test. Read the cases on the next page and write your answer in the space provided.

Exercise

Case #1

One of your team members always sits off to the side of the room—not joining the others at the table. When you try to get him to join the others, he always says he's more comfortable where he is. What should you do?

_____

_____

_____

Case #2

Your team members always wander in late. Meetings almost always start 10 to 15 minutes late because even when team members get there, they want to socialize for a minute or two. What should you do?

_____

_____

_____

Case #3

One team member always starts every discussion, always has a comment or observation after someone else speaks, and always tries to have the last word. What technique(s) can you use to deal with this team member?

_____

_____

_____

Case #4

Your team does a good job of meeting management. It holds good discussions and usually reaches agreement on decisions. However, there is very little follow through on decisions. Many of the good ideas have simply never been implemented. How should you address this?

_____

_____

_____

Case #5

You have one team member who never speaks up. Even when you use round robin, this member passes when a turn comes around. What else can you try?

_____

_____

_____

Case #6

Your team members have good discussions, but they never stick to the agenda. Often they get off on a completely different topic for the entire meeting, never making it back to the original agenda item. Since they are dealing with work-related topics, should you do anything at all? Why or why not?

_____

_____

_____

Pages 14 and 15 in the Appendix have the suggested answers to these cases.

If you've been following our instructions, you have just spent a lot of time on activities that are designed to keep your teammates involved and participating in the entire meeting process. We put all this effort into involvement techniques because it is critical that the dollars and cents spent on having that group assembled at the table be worthwhile.

Your organization is banking on the fact that putting this unique group together is going to improve the business, solve problems, and/or help carry out tasks more efficiently or effectively. Your job as team leader is to make sure that the team draws on the knowledge and experience of all members in order to make the best decisions possible.

Another important reason to focus on participation techniques to be effective relates to the point made all the way back in the Introduction: each member must feel accountable for the success of the team. How many of us can actually feel accountable for something we didn't have any input into? So, a critical task for the team leader is to make sure everyone is intimately involved in the team meetings. You can do that by conscientiously using the tools and techniques that you have just learned about. You don't have to memorize them; you don't have to become an expert overnight. This workbook should become the map that you refer to often. By the time you finish your stint as team leader, this book should be dog-eared and worn. Never be embarrassed to pull it out, even in the middle of a meeting. Everyone is still in the learning stages of teams—use all the help you have available! Sources of help include the facilitator, the sponsor, and any other books available in your organization.

One final tip:

Use a team meeting evaluation form. This form allows members to critique the meetings and suggest ways to improve. The team leader hands out the forms at the end of the meeting and tabulates the results prior to the next meeting. The entire team looks at the results and brainstorms ways to improve future meetings. This helps reinforce the idea that the responsibility for good meetings lies with all members, not just the team leader. You can find a copy of a team meeting evaluation form on page 16 of the Appendix.

CHAPTER 3

So far you have the tools for managing your meeting time and for making decisions. Now it's time for some problem-solving techniques. Because all teams—ad hoc, standing, and natural—will have to use problem-solving skills at some point or another, the discussion throughout this chapter will apply to all three.

This chapter is going to cover your role as team leader in the problem-solving process. Obviously, it will also cover some tips and techniques for problem solving. However, it is not a substitute for problem-solving training. The entire team should go through a problem-solving course that covers the full range of skills and tools for effective problem solving. If that's not possible, there are many good books on problem-solving techniques and tools that the team can use a resource. (There is a list of problem-solving books and resources on page 17 of the Appendix.) This chapter is going to help you in leading the group through the process, but it definitely doesn't cover the full range of problem-solving skills.

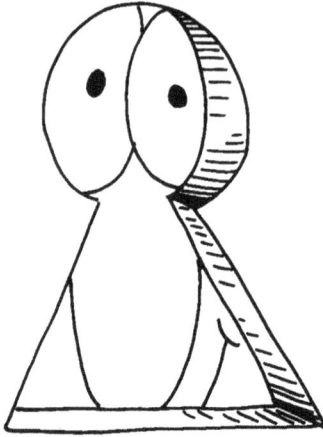

We're going to start this chapter by eavesdropping on a team meeting. The following scenario is from a customer-service team meeting. This is a natural team that is not meeting performance standards for returning customer phone calls.

Donna (the team leader): OK team, we've got to find ways to decrease the time it takes to return customer calls. Who wants to get us started?

Terry: We've got to do something about the incoming phone lines. There's simply not enough of them.

Jane: Well, we just got three new lines last March and Susie can barely answer those. How could she handle more?

Edwin: Well, I don't think it's the number of phone lines anyway. I think the problem is the computers. It takes at least five minutes to get the customer's screen up once I get the account number.

John: Have you tried using the F10 key when you're retrieving the information? I'll tell you what, that's a lot faster than the enter key!

Jane: How long is it taking us anyway? I don't really think it's that big a problem.

Terry: Well, I don't really think it's the amount of time it takes that's the real problem here. What upsets customers is the attitude that some CSRs get. Some CSRs act like they just don't care if the customer has to wait.

Donna: I don't agree—I think a lot of customers are ticked off before they even call us, and then we get blamed for having the attitude.

What went wrong with the process here? Write your comments below:

_____

_____

_____

_____

_____

_____

Compare your answers to the suggested answers on the next page.

Discussion Analysis

In this scenario, a great deal went wrong in terms of problem solving. When Donna stated the problem, it was a rather vague statement about reducing the time it takes to return calls. An improved problem statement would have been:

> It takes us an average of 2.5 hours to return a customer phone call. We need to reduce that to no more than one hour. Does everyone understand our problem statement?

In addition to an improved problem statement, this team also needed some discussion of the problem itself. Without any discussion to ensure that all members understood the problem, Terry jumped straight to a solution—"we need more phone lines." Jane then responded to Terry's idea by evaluating or judging the idea immediately. At that point, Edwin jumped in with a possible cause, and John responded with a solution to that cause. Then Jane went back to the beginning and tried to redefine the actual problem. If they continue along these lines, this team is really going to struggle with this problem.

Avoiding the Pitfalls of Problem Solving

The team fell into a common problem-solving trap: the members were mixing up problem, cause, and solution. They did not have any real method for solving their problem. Without a method, they could go in circles for the rest of the meeting. If you've ever been in a meeting like that, you know just how frustrating it can be.

The tips and techniques that we are going to cover in this chapter will help your team avoid this common pitfall and many of the other problem-solving land mines you will encounter along the way.

One of the worst problem-solving traps that a team can fall into is to confuse three very basic terms. These terms are problem, cause, and solution.

A **problem** is a discrepancy between the existing standard and the actual situation. In other words, a problem is the gap between what is desired and what has happened.

A **cause** is something that happens to lead to a problem. A cause can be acted on. If a cause is eliminated, the problem will not occur again, at least not from that cause.

A **solution** is the action we take to eliminate the cause.

This terminology may seem obvious, but it's not so much the definitions that teams get mixed up; it's *when* they should be dealing with each one. When teams bounce around between problem, solution, and cause, the result is a meeting like the previous customer-service team meeting. The checklist on the next page is the road map that is going to keep your team from getting off on that track.

Step-by-Step Checklist

✓	STEP
	Get a clear picture of the problem.
	Determine the most likely cause of the problem.
	Agree on the best solution for the cause.
	Implement the solution.
	Measure and evaluate the effectiveness of the solution.
	Be prepared to sell it to others.
	Practice continuous improvement.

STEP 1

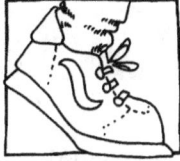

Get a Clear Picture of the Problem

Before the team can solve any problem, there must be a common understanding of just what the problem is. Taking the time to get clear, specific wording for the problem statement is the first step. The problem should be stated as the gap between the ideal situation and the actual situation and should be worded as specifically as possible.

Examples:

Our line-fill rate is currently 90 percent and we must achieve a 95 percent rate by September.

The scrap rate on line 3 is 2.3 and it must be 1.5 or below within 6 weeks.

Once you have that clear statement, a thorough discussion to ensure common understanding can eliminate many of the struggles. One way to help clarify the problem statement is to go through a "What it is, what it is not" process. Using this process, the recorder creates two columns on the flip chart. In one column, the group generates facts known about the problem. Some of those facts may tell where it occurs, what its effects are, when it occurs most, etc. The second column is a list of the things that the problem is not. These two lists can go a long way toward clarifying each team member's understanding.

Example:

Problem: Late delivery of orders	
What it is:	**What it is not:**
All truck lines	Eastern and central
Western region warehouses	region warehouses
All products	Deliveries before August 31

By going through this exercise, team members realize they must focus on the Western region warehouse and orders after August 31 in order to solve the problem.

Team members tend to get impatient with Step 1 and want to move on quickly. We all tend to be solution oriented. We don't want to take a lot of time analyzing—we want to get the problem solved and have a sense of closure. However, as the team leader, it is critical that you keep the team focused on Step 1 until you are sure that there is a common understanding of the problem. Think about it—if you can't get the team to agree on what the problem is, how in the world can you get them to agree on a solution?

Step 1 may also involve gathering some data. If team members find that they don't know the answers to the following questions, they must get answers before they can truly define the problem and move on to Step 2:

> **When does this occur?**
>
> **Where does it occur most often?**
>
> **How often does it actually occur?**
>
> **What other problems does it cause?**

What do you do if team members don't know the answers to these questions? Well, you go out and gather more information of course! There are many data-collection tools that are helpful to the team in Step 1. A simple, yet effective, method of collecting data is a checksheet. To see how to construct and use a checksheet, see page 18 of the Appendix.

Your Role as the Team Leader

Step 1 requires a lot of open discussion, so you play some important roles in Step 1. The team leader must do the following:

■ Ensure that everyone has input into the discussion by using round robin and enforcing ground rules.

■ Keep the team focused on defining the problem without jumping ahead to causes and solutions.

■ Draw out the quieter members and keep the dominant members in check.

■ Understand when and how to collect additional information.

■ Participate in the discussion as fully and openly as possible.

Exercise

Now before we move on to Step 2, how about a little practice run? Listed below you see several problem statements. Please read each one and rewrite it so that it is a specific description of the gap between the ideal situation and the existing situation. Feel free to make up details if needed.

Statement #1

Waste is sky-high! We have to get it under control.

_____

_____

_____

Statement #2

We must do something about team members who take too many breaks and stay too long.

_____

_____

_____

Statement #3

We've got to improve quality—we had 15,000 yards of rejected fabric last month!

_____

_____

_____

Statement #4

Housekeeping is terrible—if we don't get this place cleaned up, someone will get hurt.

_____

_____

_____

Turn to page 19 of the Appendix to compare your answers to our suggested answers.

STEP 2

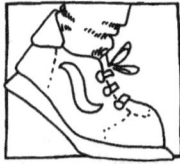

Determine the Most Likely Causes of the Problem

Once the team has a clear picture of the problem, you can move on to identifying all the possible causes. Notice there is an "s" on the end of *cause*. Most problems have multiple causes. Before the team can move on to solutions, they must identify all possible causes and narrow the options down to the most likely cause or the "root" cause.

Helpful Tool: The "Why" Technique

One simple but effective way to get at the root cause is the "why" technique. To use the "why" technique, team members simply ask "why" the problem occurs, then repeat the question after each answer until they have settled on a final or "root" cause. It usually takes asking "why" about five times to get to the root of the problem.

Example:

Why do we send out so many late shipments?
    They are not shipped out on time.

Why are the materials not shipped out on time?
    The order forms often have critical information missing.

Why is the critical information missing?
    The salespeople do not have all the necessary information at the time of order.

Why don't salespeople have all the necessary information at the time of order?

They are working in the field and do not have access to the information.

Why don't they have access to the information?

We don't have the material in written form; it's all on the computer.

The "why" technique helped uncover the root cause of the problem. Had the team members simply looked at late shipments without an analysis of the cause, they may have developed a plan for improving shipping procedures. That plan would probably not have addressed the real problem—the lack of information for the field personnel. Now that the root cause has been identified, the team is much more likely to hit on a successful solution.

Helpful Tool: Categorized Brainstorming

Categorized brainstorming is a type of brainstorming that generates ideas according to categories that are appropriate to the problem at hand. To conduct a categorized-brainstorming session, follow the phases below:

Phase 1: Write the problem (the "effect") on a flip chart.
Phase 2: Write down several categories of causes.
Phase 3: Brainstorm all possible ideas for each category.

The team can decide on the categories that are appropriate for the problem at hand. However, there are some general categories that should be considered. Office, administrative, and service teams should usually consider equipment, procedures, policies, and people. Manufacturing and engineering teams should usually consider machinery, methods, materials, and manpower.

Once the group has brainstormed all possible causes within each category, reduce each list to the most likely causes. Causes that go across more than one category should be looked at closely. The team must then reach consensus on which cause(s) to gather more data on or develop solutions for.

Helpful Tool: Clustered Brainstorming

Clustered brainstorming is another method that allows a group to combine a large number of ideas very quickly and efficiently. It can be accomplished as follows:

Phase 1: Write the problem on a flip chart.

Phase 2: Participants write down all their ideas on index cards.

Phase 3: Participants group or cluster the index cards by category.

Phase 4: Participants identify the groupings or clusters that have the greatest number of possibilities and choose the areas that warrant further analysis.

Don't forget that the rules of brainstorming apply even when using a special technique!

We have covered only a few of the tools that can be helpful in identifying root cause. There are many others that your team can learn and practice. You will find a list of problem-solving resources on page 17 of the Appendix.

Your Role as Team Leader

The role that the team leader will play in Step 2 involves the following:

■ Ensure that the team is practicing good brainstorming techniques in generating all possible causes.

■ Focus the team on root cause by using the "why" technique.

■ Keep the group from jumping ahead to a solution until it has settled on the root or most likely cause.

■ Use NGT or other rank-ordering techniques to reach consensus on which cause(s) to attack.

STEP 3

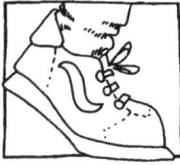

Agree on the Best Solution

Now you finally get to start the fun part—you can generate solutions! Everybody's been "chomping at the bit" to give their ideas on how to fix this problem. As the team leader, along with help from your facilitator, you've been forcing team members to define the problem clearly, carefully analyze all possible causes, and then pick the causes they want to attack. Now that you've done all that, the team can finally brainstorm all possible solutions. Remember to use the rules of brainstorming.

Once the team has brainstormed all possible options, it's time to put the consensus mind-set to work! This is where the discussion tools, such as PIN, come into play. All options are discussed and evaluated, and the team comes to consensus on the option(s) most likely to solve the problem. There's that "s" again on the end of *option*. Don't let your team fall into the trap of believing that they must settle on only one good solution. Sometimes there are several options that are not mutually exclusive—they can all be implemented!

To reach a final decision on the solution, the prioritizing tools such as NGT, 10-4, or weighted voting are critical. Consensus is key to commitment; commitment is key to successful implementation. The time spent ensuring that everyone's perspective is heard and all possible objections are dealt with will pay off in the implementation phase. A team with a solution decided upon through consensus will do what it takes to make the solution work. Sometimes it is worthwhile to run trials on the possible solutions if the team has reached a stalemate in consensus. The team simply agrees to try each solution for a certain period of time and then evaluate the outcomes. The solution with the best results becomes the final solution.

To help lead the team through Step 3, the tools that you must rely on include the following:

- The rules of brainstorming
- PIN as method of evaluating solutions
- NGT or 10-4 to narrow down options
- Consensus-building techniques to gain buy-in
- An action minutes form to commit team members to action
- A measurement planning form to develop a plan to measure outcomes

STEP 4

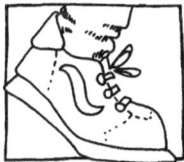

Implement the Solution

Once the team settles on a particular option or options, you must develop a plan of action. No matter how great the solution is, it does no good unless the team makes it a reality. As part of Step 3, the team must make assignments and set specific time frames for things to happen. All of these actions must be written down on the action minutes form and then followed up.

You're asking yourself right now—isn't this step obvious? Of course it is! However, teams sometimes lose steam at this point. They feel such a sense of accomplishment from Steps 1 through 3, they may feel as if they're finished! Who can blame them—they've labored over the problem statement, carefully analyzed the causes and chosen one to focus on, and struggled to reach consensus on the best solution. It seems like they should be done, especially if they've hit on what seems to be the perfect solution. They just want to celebrate and get back to everyday business.

However, if you let them fizzle out now, all that hard work is for nothing. We covered some simple rules in Chapter 1 for following up on action plans. Let's quickly review those tips:

- Use the action minutes form to record the specifics of the action item (what the assignment is, who took responsibility, and when it is to be completed).

- When there will be a long period of time between meetings, follow up face-to-face with team members who have assignments.

- Break up responsibilities and have more than one person involved whenever possible.

- If members seem to be having trouble carrying out assignments, find out if additional resources are needed or what you can do to help.

Additional Implementation Tips

If the team decides to conduct trials on several options, there may be a fairly long period of time with no required meetings. Schedule short check-up meetings during this period. These meetings won't take long—information-sharing meetings are short. However, these short meetings will help motivate members with assignments to follow through.

Keep charts or tables with information about project status posted in public places. When team members see the information frequently, it will serve as a reminder and help keep the commitment to implementation high.

STEP 5

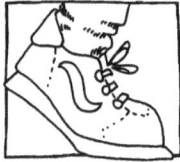

Measure and Evaluate the Effectiveness of the Solution

Unfortunately, even when you follow this process, things may go wrong. The team may not have hit on the best solution, outside factors may have kept it from being successful, or it may be successful but simply need some "tweaking." In Step 5, the team evaluates the success of the solution by comparing data from before and after. If the team members are satisfied that the outcomes are successful, they celebrate and share the information with other parts of the organization or other teams who might benefit. If the outcomes don't meet the criteria for success, the team goes back to Step 2 or 3 and repeats the process. If it looks like the team acted on the wrong cause, it should go back to the list of possible causes and repeat Steps 3 and 4 on the next most likely cause. However, if the solution seems to be the problem, the team should revisit the possible solutions and select another option.

The team sets the stage for evaluation by setting measures in place. Once the solution is decided upon, the team must decide who will measure the outcomes, how often it will be measured, and what the time frame will be. Many teams have found the following table to be a very effective mechanism for recording those decisions.

Measurement Planning Table Example	
What will be measured?	Number and type of mistakes
How will it be measured?	Check sheets at workstation
Who will be responsible?	Each operator for his or her machine
How long will it be measured?	120 days
What will be considered success?	Reduce mistakes by 60%

Note: The table can have as many columns as needed. The number of measures decided upon determines the number of columns. Typical measures include customer satisfaction, number of defects, scrap, cycle time, inventory, on-time deliveries, etc.

Your Role as Team Leader

The skills required of the team leader in Step 5 include the following:

- Evaluate data.
- Lead the group back through the process if necessary.
- Keep the team focused on the outcome and potential for final success.
- Keep enthusiasm high—a cheerleader!

A Final Note

Once all the measures are in and final decisions are made, publish the results. When commitments are made publicly, people are more likely to follow through for the long term. It is likely that this problem-solving effort resulted in changes in the way things are done. It can be tough to change old habits. When the initial excitement of solving the problem wears off, people may revert to the old ways of doing things, causing the problem to rear its ugly head again. Publicizing the results makes it a little tougher for people to fall back on their old ways. Continuing to measure the new performance is another mechanism for maintaining the momentum. Keeping up with a measurement system can serve as a reminder to practice the new method until it becomes habit.

STEP 6

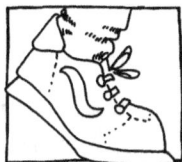

Be Prepared to Sell It

Unfortunately, not everyone is as high on the idea, recommendation, or change as the team is. The team members believe wholeheartedly in this solution/idea/recommendation because of their history with it. However, there are others who will be affected by this change—and they don't have the benefit of having been through what the team has been through. The burden of selling the solution falls on the team. Forgetting to sell it to others may make the difference between final success or failure.

Sometimes Step 6 actually comes before Step 5. If the solution decided upon falls outside the team's boundaries, other key people may have to be convinced before implementation of the idea. Or the team may find that the solution is so useful that other areas could benefit from it. Regardless of the reason for selling the idea, the basic selling is the same. There are a couple of pointers that can help teams "turn others on" to the idea/solution.

KEY #1

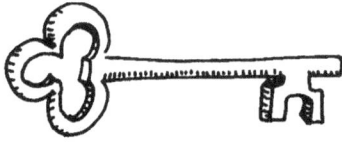

Anticipate all possible questions and be prepared with solid answers.

To accomplish this, the team should brainstorm all possible questions, objections, or concerns that could arise from this recommendation. Once that list has been compiled, the questions are assigned to specific team members to prepare initial responses. These responses are presented to the team for critique and improvement.

KEY #2

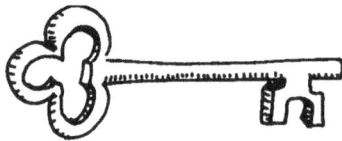

Present in terms of what implementation will do for the company.

The team is much more likely to gain the attention of managers by presenting how this solution will benefit the company or the customer. That's not to say that no one cares if the change makes life easier for the employees; however, the real attention-getter is how it benefits the company/customer. One of the best ways to show benefits is with a cost-benefit analysis. This analysis can show how the potential savings or benefits outweigh the expense of a proposed improvement. To complete a cost-benefit analysis, the team goes through the following stages:

Stage 1: Calculate the known costs associated with the proposed solution. Include the cost of new equipment, manpower, and other associated costs.

Stage 2: Calculate the potential benefit of the proposed solution. Benefits could include factors such as increased productivity, decreased rework, reduced costs, and improved customer satisfaction. Some benefits repeat year after year. If this is the case, the benefit should be calculated over the life of the solution.

Stage 3: The net benefit is the difference between the estimated costs and benefits.

Example:

The team decides on a new piece of equipment that will reduce scrap by 10%, for an annual savings of $10,000 over the next 5 years ($50,000). The equipment will cost $16,000 plus $7,000 in wiring and installation. The net benefit is $27,000.

Calculate the cost-benefit for the following case:

You are the team leader of a team charged with identifying problems with the billing system and recommending changes. The team has developed a proposal to reduce billing expenses. The plan includes the purchase and installation of three new computers and training the 12 employees in the department on use of the new program and equipment.

The costs associated with the recommendation are as follows:

3 computers and peripherals	$7,500
1 laser printer	$2,200
software expense	$1,500
installation	$ 750
1 half-day training session	$1,200

The estimated results in terms of savings are as follows:

Decreased order processing time by 50%
(current processing costs: $150,000)

Decreased billing errors by 20%
(current cost of fixing billing errors: $25,000)

Based on the information above, calculate the cost-benefit of this project over the next 5 years.

_____

_____

_____

_____

_____

To check your answer, see page 20 of the Appendix.

KEY #3

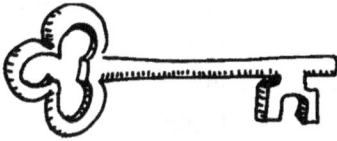

Make sure you have the right people assembled.

People can be very territorial within the workplace. It is important to invite anyone who is impacted by a decision to the presentation. There's no better way to kill the project before it even begins than to leave out a manager or supervisor in an area that will have to support the team in the implementation. To help develop a list of people to invite to the presentation, the team should consider the following questions:

- Who/what department will be impacted by this decision/ change?
- Who/what department is the supplier in this process?
- Who/what department is the customer in this process?
- Who has a strong interest in this process?
- Who will benefit from an improvement in this area?

Not all questions will apply to your project. Use those that apply, and the answers should help you compile a list of people to invite to the presentation. You may also want to get your sponsor involved in developing this list.

STEP 7

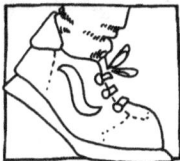

Practice Continuous Improvement

Unfortunately, solving existing problems is only one small part of an overall mind-set that has to be in place for your organization to be successful. All organizations have to constantly strive for continuous improvement in their processes, in their customer service, and in their thinking. Today's highly competitive environment means that there is no such thing as good enough. Even if your customer is satisfied today, their needs could change at the drop of a hat. Through continuous improvement, teams can be prepared to meet those changing needs.

Both standing teams and natural teams will have many opportunities for continuous improvement. As a matter of fact, one of the reasons for forming natural teams is continuous improvement! Since ad hoc teams disband once they have met their objective, the following discussion does not apply to ad hoc teams.

Three Critical Tools of Continuous Improvement

The Quality Grid

To practice continuous improvement, team members must know what they are doing, what they should be doing, and what they should improve upon. The quality grid is an excellent tool for answering those questions.

The quality grid consists of two dimensions: "what you do" and "how you do it." The "what you do" dimension includes two categories: right things and wrong things. The "how you do it" dimension also has two categories: things done wrong and things done right. When you put it all together, it looks like this:

	How You Do It	
What You Do	Right Things Wrong	Right Things Right
	Wrong Things Wrong	Wrong Things Right

Plugging their activities into the four quadrants can be an eye-opening experience for team members. They can identify the things they should stop doing altogether (wrong things right or wrong things wrong), what they should continue to monitor and measure (right things right), and where the opportunities for improvement are (right things wrong). Once the opportunities are identified, the team can get back into a problem-solving mode and methodically attack each area.

Flow Chart

Another useful tool for continuous improvement is the flow chart. The flow chart provides any team with good information about where bottlenecks exist, where work or rework can be eliminated, and where time can be saved. Teams should routinely pick an activity and flow chart it in order to identify the opportunities for improvement. Thorough understanding of the steps of each activity in a process allows the team to identify potential problems and act on each one before it turns into a full-scale problem.

To complete a flow chart, the team goes through the following stages:

Stage 1: Break down the work into a logical sequence of events—put each of these steps into activity boxes with arrows indicating the flow of steps.

Stage 2: Look at each of the activity boxes and determine where decisions are made (checkpoints). Indicate decision points with diamond shapes.

Stage 3: If a yes/no option is available at the decision point, there must be two arrows. One arrow indicates the next step of the process if the answer is yes, and one indicates the next step of the process if the answer is no.

Stage 4: Place the beginning and ending of the process in ovals.

Example:

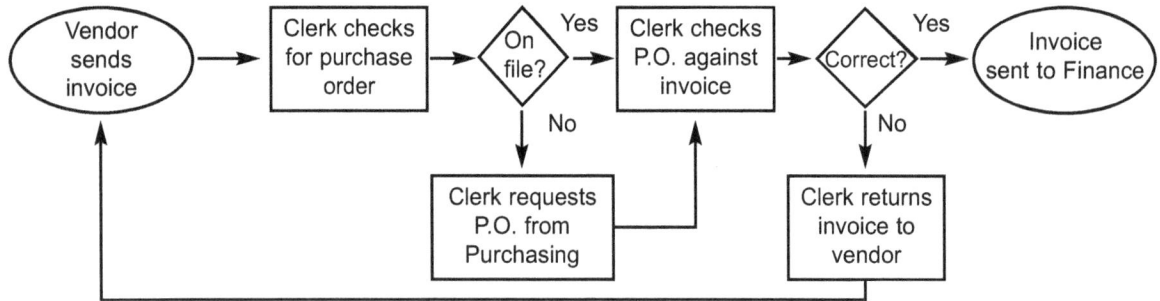

Assignment

Meet with your team and choose an activity to flow chart. Follow the step-by-step method for constructing a flow chart for one process that your team is responsible for. Make note of the points in the process that slow down activity (bottlenecks). Identify points where errors are most likely to occur. As a team, determine your next step for improving your process.

Contingency Diagram

A contingency diagram is a useful tool for preventing problems. To use the contingency diagram, select a situation that the team has identified as having strong potential for problems. Draw a diagram like the example on the next page and write the potential problem situation in the oval. Brainstorm all the actions that could cause this problem to occur (remember your rules of brainstorming here). The problems are listed on the arrows pointing toward the problem situation as shown. The next step is to develop a list of actions that would prevent the problem (the opposite of the actions written on the arrows). This list is used to develop a checklist of activities that becomes the team's plan for prevention.

Some team members save on CDs

No method for naming files

Some team members don't think files need to be saved

No back-up server

Problem

Losing computer files

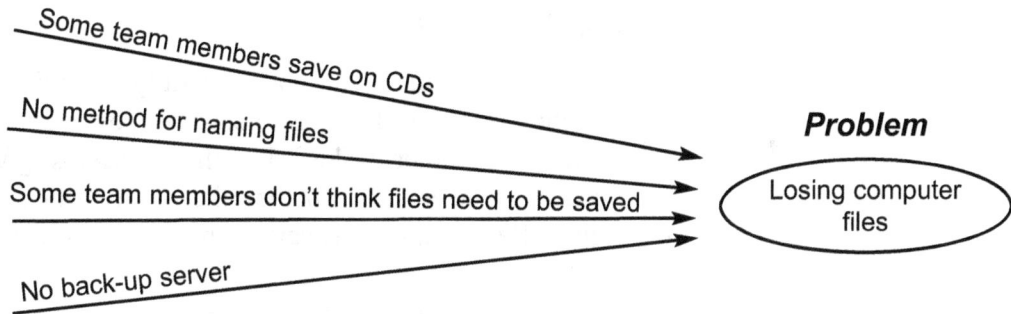

The checklist below is the opposite of what is written on the lines above. It is an action plan for prevention.

Prevention Checklist

✓ **Develop policies on what should be saved and where.**

✓ **Develop a method for naming files and communicate this to all team members.**

✓ **Install a back-up server and assign to one team member as a weekly task.**

Develop Measures to Track Continuous Improvement

N

Improvement is not possible without measures. Teams must have a standard to begin with before that standard can be raised. We have talked about the importance of developing measures for short-term goals throughout Chapters 1 and 2. However, natural teams won't always have short-term goals to focus on. It is critical for the team to have meaningful measures of their day-to-day performance. Without measures and solid baseline data, teams simply have to guess at whether they are doing the "right things right." Measures might include on-time deliveries, number of units produced, percentage of scrap, number of hours of rework, etc.

Assignment

Meet with your team and carefully examine all measures currently in place. Do these measures cover critical activities in meeting customer needs? Do the measures give information needed to determine whether the team is doing "right things right"? Based on the answers to the questions, determine whether your performance measures need to be added to, deleted, or modified. Develop proposed measures, as well as methods of tracking those measures, and present them to your sponsor. Once you have approval on your new measures, determine how you will track, record, and use those measures in your continuous improvement journey.

Summary

We have covered a lot of information in Chapter 3. One important thing to remember is you don't have to remember. You will not be expected to become an expert overnight. This workbook is intended as a reference book—something you pull out whenever you need it. The rest of the team knows that you are a team member just like them. It won't bother anybody if you pull out this book for help.

Additional Tips

Rely on your facilitator; he or she is a neutral bystander who is not participating in the process, making it easier to help with the process itself.

If you can't have your facilitator at the meeting, assign someone on the team to be the process coach—the process coach simply has the written description of the tool in front of him/her and prompts the group through the process.

DIVE

To help team members remember the phases of the process, use some kind of reminder. We use the acronym *DIVE:*

Phase 1: **D**efine the problem.
Phase 2: **I**dentify the causes.
Phase 3: **V**erify the solution.
Phase 4: **E**valuate and adjust.

This acronym covers each of the critical aspects of problem solving in one little word. The "V" may be a stretch, but it does work. By thinking about it as the DIVE approach, the team can use the following saying to remember the phases of problem solving: when we have a problem, just dive in!

Post the phases of problem solving on a chart that everyone can see. If the team likes DIVE, great! Put it up for all to remember. If the team just wants to write out phase 1, phase 2, etc., fine; put that on the chart. Just post it as a reminder.

Last but not least. . .

Hang in there! Don't become discouraged and don't let the team lose faith! Problem solving is tough, but it pays off for everybody in the long run with improved processes, less rework, reduced errors, and better customer service.

CHAPTER 4

Throughout the life of the team, a team leader will probably have the "opportunity" to deal with several different types of conflicts. Let's take a look at three types of conflict.

Type 1 Conflict

Handling Interpersonal Conflicts between Individual Team Members

Type 2 Conflict

Part A—Resolving Different Points of View on the Team

Part B—Resolving Conflicts from Team to Team

Type 3 Conflict

Dealing with Conflict between Yourself and a Member

Each of these types of conflicts requires a unique approach. This chapter will take you through each type of conflict.

Type 1

Conflict

Handling Interpersonal Conflicts between Individual Team Members

It's a fact of life: you will find yourself in situations where two people simply do not like each other or have personalities that clash. In a traditional organization, conflicts are often avoided by people avoiding each other. However, a team environment doesn't allow for that avoidance. People must work together to accomplish the team's goal. The key to managing these interpersonal conflicts is to get the issues out on the table and involve the conflicting team members in coming up with a mutually acceptable resolution. Let's look at how you accomplish that, step-by-step.

Step-by-Step Checklist

✓	STEP
	Surface the conflict.
	Have each member define the issue/problem as he or she sees it and check for understanding.
	Identify the behaviors that must change in order to eliminate the issue/problem.
	Develop an action plan.
	Follow up.

STEP 1

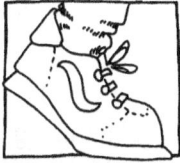

Surface the Conflict

Often conflict in an organization is not outright. Obviously, people don't normally scream at each other or call each other names in the workplace (at least, not very often). Usually conflict between individuals shows up camouflaged as sarcastic comments, closed or hostile body language, constant disagreements of opinion, or, as mentioned earlier, avoidance. Very often, it is up to the team leader to set up a meeting between these individuals and open the discussion by "laying the cards out on the table." To accomplish this, you must be willing to use direct language and come straight to the point. You must also be as specific as possible in your description of the situation or behaviors. Let's look at an example of a team leader opening a discussion with two team members who have been "sniping" at each other in team meetings, sending negative signals with body language, and blocking team decisions with their conflicting opinions.

Team Leader: I feel that we may be having some problems in our team meetings. How do you two feel about it?

Team Member 1: Everything seems fine to me. We've always got an agenda, we start on time, and we get out on time. I don't see any problems.

Team Member 2: What kind of problems are you talking about?

Team Leader: I don't know—it just doesn't seem like we always do such a good job making decisions. What do you think?

This team leader is beating around the bush. The opening sentence did not focus the members on the problem at hand. By opening with team meetings in general, the team leader gave the members an opportunity to avoid the issue. The second statement about decision-making skills will again give the members an opening to discuss all aspects of decision-making other than their behavior toward each other. The following example is direct, to the point, and specifies the behaviors that are contributing to conflict.

Team Leader: I would like to talk about some things that I have noticed in our team meetings recently. Often when one of you is speaking, the other rolls his eyes, takes a big sigh, or throws his head back. I have also heard comments under your breath, and occasionally there have been little barbs thrown back and forth. I'd like to talk about this because I believe others have noticed it as well and it is beginning to affect our meeting productivity.

This time the team leader gave a specific description of the problem behaviors. The team members are not going to be able to avoid the real issue with this opening.

The following exercise will allow you to practice your skills in surfacing the conflict.

On the next two pages, there are three situations that a team leader might face.

Exercise

Read each situation and write an opening statement to surface the conflict.

1. You are the leader of a natural team with two team members who are always talking to other team members about the other one. Each one believes that the other one does not do his/her share of the work, both on the work floor and in team assignments. However, they won't talk to each other about it. How should you open your conflict resolution session?

_____

_____

_____

2. You are the leader of a project team. The team has a very short time frame. There are two members who are always blocking decisions. You use nominal group technique to narrow down options, but these two members always seem to get stuck on two different ideas and neither one will back down. They often take up most of the team meeting debating about the option each one supports. How should you open your conflict resolution session?

_____

_____

_____

3. You are the team leader of a standing team that has just changed membership due to rotation. One member of the original team has already developed a strong dislike for one of the new members. They often interrupt each other during team meetings and try to talk over each other. Your facilitator does a good job of enforcing the ground rules and usually gets them to stop, but then they each seem to sit back and "check out" for the remainder of the meeting. How should you open your conflict resolution session?

_____

_____

_____

See pages 21 and 22 of the Appendix to compare your answers to the suggested answers.

Two more points about Step 1. First, make sure that you set up this meeting somewhere that is private and does not allow for distractions or interruptions. It is important to keep these two members focused through the entire process. Second, and related to the first point, ensure that all members have set aside an adequate amount of time for this session. You don't want to get started with the conflict-resolution process and then have to leave before it can be completed. Get agreement beforehand on a reasonable time period that all members can commit to. Typically, a session like this will take an hour or more.

STEP 2

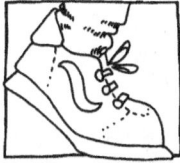

Define the Problem/Issue

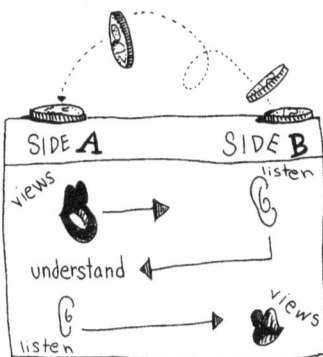

In Step 2, each member expresses how he or she views the issue. It is important to remember that the purpose of Step 2 is to seek understanding, not agreement. Each team member states his or her views and feelings. You will have plenty of opportunity to practice your questioning skills during this step since members will probably need help expressing themselves.

After the first member has completed presenting his or her views, the team leader asks the other team member to paraphrase and summarize to show understanding. After all, it doesn't help to express views if the other person doesn't get what you are saying. Once there is complete understanding of one side of the issue, the other member has his or her chance to speak. During this step, the team leader may have to play a strong role, ensuring that each side has the chance to speak without interruption.

STEP 3

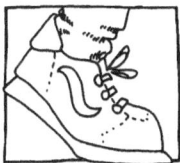

Identify the Behaviors that Must Change

The purpose of Step 2 was to understand the two views of the conflicting parties. The purpose of Step 3 is to try to find ways to bring those conflicting views closer. To accomplish this, the two members must identify the behaviors that keep the conflict alive and kicking. The way to accomplish this is to go through a "start, stop, continue" exercise. Using a flip chart or a form, each member develops a list of behaviors that he or she could begin to

practice in order to address the conflict—the "start" list. Each member also develops a list of the behaviors that he or she should "stop" displaying in order to resolve the issue. The last list each member develops is a list of the behaviors to "continue"—behaviors that aren't causing problems. Remember: Each member is making a list of what *he or she* should do, not what the *other person* should do.

After the individual lists are completed, the members look at each other's lists and determine whether these actions or behaviors will help resolve the conflict. Each member may make suggestions about additions or deletions on the other's list. Remind the members that the lists do not have to be perfect—they do not have to address all behaviors. What we're looking for with this first list is a *start* in the direction of resolution.

STEP 4

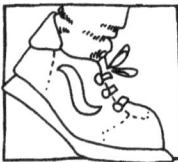

Develop an Action Plan

Step 4 is simply a matter of taking the behaviors that are listed on the "start, stop, continue" lists and turning them into action statements. For example, if one of the behaviors on the "stop" list is interrupting when the other person is speaking, the action item becomes:

> I will wait until I am certain that Joe has completed his sentence before I speak up.

The team members work together to develop an action plan for each behavior. The team leader simply helps lead them through the discussion and keep them on task. In addition to action items, the team members agree on a means of reminding each other of the commitments. They can use nonverbal reminders like hand signals or one-word simple reminders.

STEP 5

Follow Up

At the end of Step 4, the team members must decide how frequently they will meet to talk about how the changes are working, what other changes are needed, and how to continue to improve their interactions. Remember, we said in Step 3 that we weren't trying to address all problematic behaviors; we were simply trying to get started in the right direction. The major purpose of these follow-up meetings is to evaluate the success of the agreements and make any needed "tweaks." If the team members have had some success in reducing the conflicts, they may also want to deal with any additional issues or behaviors. If that's the case, go back to the original "start, stop, continue" lists and take the same approach as the first go-round.

Additional Tips

The first few times you try this approach, have a facilitator help you through it. We can all use help in dealing with emotional issues.

Keep team members focused on behaviors—not personality traits.

Think of yourself as the traffic cop who is controlling the process. Don't get caught up in the content of the conflict; just help guide the team members through the step-by-step process.

Type 2

Conflict

Part A—Resolving Different Points of View on the Team

Unfortunately, this is another reality of teams: sometimes factions develop within the team. A problem or issue will come up, and the team will develop two or even three factions, each supporting a different solution. Avoiding or ignoring this situation can result in the teamwork breaking down in many other areas. Let's look at the checklist of activities for dealing with this type of conflict.

Step-by-Step Checklist

✓	STEP
	Define the needs of each side of the issue.
	Brainstorm all options for addressing the issue.
	Determine criteria for choosing options based on the needs of both sides.
	Select an option.
	Develop an action plan.
	Evaluate the outcomes.

STEP 1

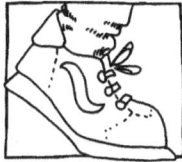

Define the Needs of Each Side of the Issue

Needs versus Solutions

Before we discuss how to do this, let's discuss what we mean by *needs*. *Conflicts* are usually defined as conflicting solutions—setting up a win-lose situation. Let's take a look at an example:

> A team of employees share office space. One faction of the team wants the window open; the other wants the window closed. This situation is win-lose, right? If one group of employees get what they want, the other group can't possibly get their way.

This conflict has been defined in terms of solution. If you asked either side of this issue to redefine the conflict in terms of need, you might hear "We need the window closed" or "We need the window open"—still a win-lose situation. To get to the real need, you must find out why each side has proposed that solution. The advantages that solution has for them is where the real need lies.

Why do we need to define the conflict in terms of needs? In our example, there's no chance of a win-win situation—the window is closed or open. Each side might compromise and open it halfway, but then neither side is happy. This win-lose approach to conflict goes against everything involved in developing a successful team. However, if each side stated needs such as "We need fresh air" or "We need to avoid drafts that blow papers around," they may be able to come up with other alternatives. Stating the conflict in terms of solutions limits the possibilities to two. Stating the conflict in terms of needs opens up all kinds of new possibilities. Only by understanding the needs can the team come up with solutions that meet the needs of both sides.

So how do you accomplish Step 1? It's actually quite easy. Each side of the issue states its members' needs. Members of Side A state their needs with members of Side B, listening until they have a complete understanding. Members of Side B must demonstrate that understanding by summarizing and paraphrasing Side A's needs. A recorder captures the key points after both sides are satisfied that there is complete understanding (understanding—not agreement!).

Sometimes a member of the group will try to sneak in a solution disguised as a need. When this happens, the team leader or facilitator gets at the need by asking why the team member believes that solution is the best. The answer to that question should uncover the need.

Members of Side B then have an opportunity to present their needs with Side A summarizing and paraphrasing. Again, the recorder captures the key points after both sides are satisfied that there is complete understanding. Once the two lists of needs are developed, the lists are set aside to be used later in the process.

Note: If there are more than two sides involved in the conflict, you simply repeat Step 1 until all the sides of the issue have had an opportunity to state their needs.

STEP 2

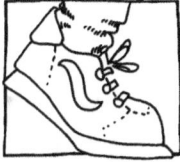

Brainstorm All Options for Addressing the Issue

Since you and your team members have had a lot of practice brainstorming, Step 2 is easy. All members are involved in this step—brainstorming together as a team helps pull everyone back into a team mind-set. The rules of brainstorming apply—the recorder writes down all ideas and no one evaluates or judges ideas. Once all ideas are captured, the team goes back through the list to discuss and ensure understanding of all options. At this stage, we are not looking for agreement on the options, just understanding. Don't let the team members criticize or judge the ideas—limit the discussion to clarifying questions.

STEP 3

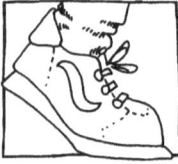

Determine Criteria for Choosing Options

This is where the lists of needs come back into the picture. Now that the team members have come up with several options, they must develop a means of choosing the best one. Without criteria for that choice, team members may fall right back into arguing for their original solution. The needs that were listed in Step 1 dictate the criteria. Team members revisit that list of needs, discuss each, and determine which needs are most important. They may rank order the needs, or they may pick one or two that are critical. Those critical or highly ranked needs then become the criteria for choosing the best option from the brainstormed list.

Let's take a look at our previous example. Remember the team members who were sharing office space? One side wanted the window open, and the other side wanted it closed. The team members stated their needs: one faction stated a need for fresh air, and the other faction stated a need to keep drafts away. Those needs now become the criteria for evaluating the options. The option that provides fresh air without creating drafts will be the win-win solution.

STEP 4

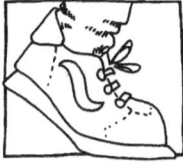

Select an Option

The option chosen must meet at least one need of each side. So before team members even begin to try to select an option from the brainstormed list, they must strike any option that does not meet at least one need of both sides. Be sure that team members don't just start striking options they don't like; only options that truly do not meet any of the needs of one of the sides should be struck in this phase.

Once the team members have examined the list and eliminated options if necessary, the next step is to rank order the list. They may use the 10-4 method or the rank order method (allotting points for options). Each member makes his or her decision on rankings individually. The recorder captures and sums the individual scores to determine team preference. The team members discuss the options receiving the greatest scores and reach final consensus on the option or options to implement. If there are options that are not mutually exclusive, implementing several may meet more of the needs of both sides.

STEP 5

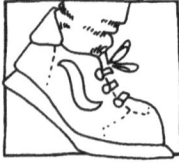

Develop an Action Plan

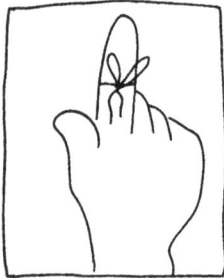

Once both sides have agreed on an option to proceed with, the team must develop a plan for implementation. Individual team members must take responsibility for specific assignments with target dates for completion. Whenever possible, each member should have an assigned action item. If that's not possible or practical, be particularly careful to ensure that some members from both sides of the issue have assignments. Remember to use the action form and write down the assignments. Things that are written are less likely to be forgotten.

STEP 6

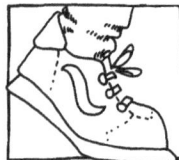

Evaluate the Options

At the end of the meeting, the team should have a brief discussion of the process. A round-robin discussion works well, with each member telling briefly how he or she thinks the process worked, one thing that he or she thought went well, and one thing that could be improved for next time. After this round robin, the team must set a time to get together again to evaluate the success of the chosen option(s) and make any necessary adjustments. Ensure that the team allows enough time to elapse before the next meeting to be able to evaluate the long-term effectiveness of the solution. However, try to avoid scheduling the meeting so far in the future that it is forgotten about. A good rule of thumb is no more than six weeks and no less than three weeks between the resolution session and the follow-up meeting.

Type 2

Conflict

Part B—Resolving Conflicts from Team to Team

On occasion, conflicts arise between two different teams. They may be natural teams that work in the same area, or ad hoc or standing teams working on related issues. Regardless of the type of team, the effect of conflicts can be detrimental to team productivity. The conflict itself can begin to override the team's purpose. Before the conflict gets out of hand, the team leader or the facilitator must bring the teams together to surface and resolve the issue.

On the next page is the checklist for accomplishing this. This checklist might look familiar—Steps 3 through 8 are on the checklist for Part A—Resolving Different Points of View on the Team. Therefore, we will just discuss the first two steps.

Step-by-Step Checklist

✓	STEP
	Arrange a meeting between the teams involved in conflict.
	Schedule a facilitator to help the teams through the resolution process.
	Define the needs of each side of the issue.
	Brainstorm all options for addressing the issue.
	Determine criteria for choosing options based on the needs of both sides.
	Select an option.
	Develop an action plan.
	Evaluate the outcomes.

STEP 1

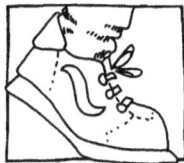

Arrange a Meeting Between the Teams

Step 1 may be a little tricky. If we're talking about setting up a meeting with your own team, you certainly have the authority as team leader to do that. However, when we start talking about other teams, other areas, and other sponsors, you may not feel as comfortable with approaching the team. A lot depends on the culture of your organization. Some companies have been successful in setting an environment in which any team member feels empowered to arrange a meeting if it will solve a problem, address an issue, or improve business. Other companies still have a more formal structure, requiring approvals by managers or supervisors.

If you feel at all uncomfortable with the idea of approaching the team leader or sponsor of the other team, this is one of those times to turn to your sponsor for help. Go to your sponsor and ask him or her to help you arrange this meeting. There are a couple of ways to approach this. You and the sponsor might go to the sponsor of the other team together. Or, the sponsor may decide that the best approach is for him or her to meet alone with the other sponsor. Trust your sponsor on this one: he or she probably knows which approach will be most effective.

Once the meeting has the "blessings" of all sponsors, coordinate scheduling with the other team leader. The meeting time should accommodate both teams' schedules and should allow an adequate amount of time—one to two hours. Depending on the size of the two teams, you may also have to decide who will attend the meeting. If including all members of both teams will result in a meeting of more than 10 to 12 people, the teams should choose representatives to participate in the meeting. If you do have to structure the meeting this way, each team must be allowed the same number of representatives.

STEP 2

Schedule a Facilitator

A sense of fairness is very important to all the members involved in conflicts. For this reason, we strongly suggest that neither of the team leaders try to lead the two teams through the conflict resolution process. If one or the other leads the process, that leaves one team feeling as if the other was given an unfair advantage. Therefore rely on a facilitator. The facilitator is not involved in the conflict, is not part of either team, and is more likely to be seen as unbiased or neutral. As a matter of fact, if possible, try to arrange for a facilitator who does not usually work with either of the two teams involved in the conflict. This will ensure that neither team feels as if the other had an advantage.

Now it's time to backtrack. Remember Steps 3 through 8 are exactly the same as Steps 1 through 6 for conflict within the team. So go back to pages 4-11–16 and reread the steps for team conflict before you participate in the process. Even though you are not leading the process, others on your team look to you for direction.

You must be able to model the expected behaviors and encourage others to participate in the process. The team members will take their lead from you. If you are careful to state the conflict in terms of needs, refrain from criticizing ideas, and look for creative ways to meet the needs of both sides, then team members are likely to do so as well.

Type 3

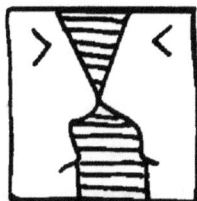

Conflict

Resolving Conflicts Between Yourself and a Team Member

Unfortunately, you are likely to find yourself caught up in conflict with another team member at some point. As the team leader, you must model the behaviors that are expected from other team members. You must be willing to deal with conflict as an opportunity for growth and improvement. You have to be willing to confront the conflict head-on. And you must be willing to deal with conflict with a positive approach. So, now that you know you have to be the perfect role model when it comes to conflict, let's go over the method that will help you do just that.

Step-by-Step Checklist

✓	STEP
	Surface the issue.
	Gain all information/views of the other side.
	Review points of agreement.
	Give your views.
	Work together to develop an action plan you can both agree to.
	Evaluate the outcomes.

We will carefully go through this process, step-by-step.

STEP 1

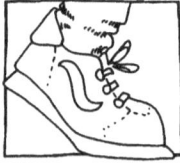

Surface the Issue

We have already discussed dealing with conflict between team members. However, this time it's a little different. This time *you* are involved in conflict. You will have to be discreet when dealing with the other person involved in the conflict. If you are too direct in the manner in which you surface the issue, you may set off some defensive alarms for the other person. This is not to say you dance around the issue, but if you open up by stating your view of the problem, Step 2 is not going to go well. Your goal in Step 2 is to hear the other person's views of the issue, and if you open with your own view, Step 2 will be the other person's defense against your view instead of their own view. For the remainder of the process to be successful, you must open with the general topic or issue that you would like to discuss and avoid any statement that communicates your view of the issue.

Wrong Way: I would like to talk about the problems you are having in meetings.

This first example expresses the team leader's opinion that the other person is creating problems in team meetings.

Right Way: I would like to talk about how you and I are interacting during team meetings.

This example simply states the issue that needs to be discussed without indicating the team leader's view of who or what is at fault.

STEP 2

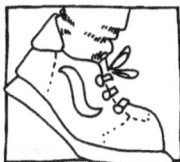

Gain All Information/Views of the Other Side

In Step 2, you will have a chance to practice your questioning skills. Any time you open your mouth during Step 2, the only purpose should be to ask a question, seek clarification, or indicate understanding. Step 2 should be one of the longest steps in the process. Ensure that you have a full and complete understanding of how the other person views the situation. Also ensure that the other person has shared all his or her views on the issue. Your major goal in Step 2 is to experience fully the feelings and views of the other side of the issue.

STEP 3

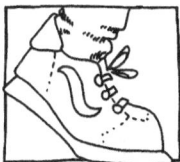

Review Points of Agreement

Step 3 is critical. If you jump right into giving your views after listening to the views of the other person, he or she may feel like you didn't hear any of it—you were just waiting to take your turn talking. So make sure you never skip this important step. In Step 3, you restate the points that the other person has made that you agree with. If you have done your job in listening with empathy, tried to put yourself in the other person's shoes, and

looked for points of agreement, you should be able to find some common ground. Unfortunately, we sometimes listen to others for the purpose of developing our own argument. You cannot do that if you expect this process to be successful. If you have truly listened and you still can't find any substance that you agree with, you may be able to agree to some of the circumstances that led to the other person's views.

Example: "I can understand how you feel that I sometimes cut off your input."

This statement does not necessarily show agreement, but it does show understanding.

STEP 4

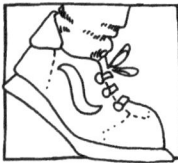

Give Your Views

You have set the stage for the other person to listen to you by actively listening to him or her. You have also reduced the chances of defensiveness by showing that you do have some areas you can agree on. Now the task is to give your views, using very specific, clear wording. Much of what you have to say should be driven by what you heard and understood in Step 2. However, if you view things differently than the other person, now is the time to speak up. As you state your views, you should use specific, accurate terms rather than fuzzy terms.

Example:

Fuzzy
"When you disrupt the meeting"

Specific
"When you continue talking after the gatekeeper has tried to bring the team back to the subject at hand"

You must also be careful to limit the description to observable behaviors. Avoid words such as *never, always,* and *constantly.* Leave out any inferences about why the person does this or inferences about his or her character. Here are two examples of how *not* to do it:

Example:

"You don't care about the other team members' views."
(inference about character)

"You are always interrupting other people."
(use of the word always*)*

You must also clearly describe the effect of the person's behaviors. State these effects clearly and concisely.

Example:

"Our meetings take longer than they have to and we don't always complete the agenda."

Step 4 should be the shortest step in the process. Simply state your views that differ from the other team member's, check to ensure understanding, and move on to Step 5.

On the following page is an exercise for you to practice giving your views.

Improve the statements listed below by following the rules for giving your views. Make up details if needed to improve the statement.

"When you come on so strong in the team meeting, everybody else just shuts down. You don't seem to think that anybody else has anything useful to say."

_____

_____

_____

"You're always late to every single meeting we have. You don't have any consideration for other team members' time."

_____

_____

_____

"I don't think you care if this team succeeds in solving our problem. No matter what I do to try to get you to take responsibility for your action items, you never follow up."

_____

_____

_____

"When you constantly ignore the ground rules of the team, other members feel like they can break them too. We've got to work on this!"

_____

_____

_____

See page 23 of the Appendix to compare your ideas to the suggested answers.

STEP 5

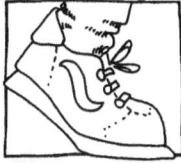

Work Together to Develop an Action Plan

At this phase of the process, the two of you must pull together to come up with an action plan that you can both agree on. Your tone in Step 5 should be very matter of fact, conveying the attitude that it is now time to work together. Where Step 2 consisted of receiving information and Steps 3 and 4 consisted of sending information, Step 5 should be two-way communication. Both members should be actively involved in coming up with creative ideas that can address the difference of views. You should continue to use active listening skills and to express your views clearly. Generate as many options as possible and then agree on those that are most likely to address your issue. Once you agree on what that action is, both must agree to specific responsibilities and the timeline for follow-up.

STEP 6

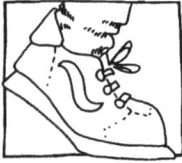

Evaluate the Outcomes

There are three good reasons to evaluate the outcomes. The first is to make any necessary adjustments. You don't always hit on the perfect solution with the first try—as a matter of fact, you rarely do. The evaluation step ensures that any needed adjustments are made so that we don't end up right back where we started. A second reason for the evaluation stage is to continuously improve the way conflicts are managed. Learning to use this process takes practice. No one will become an expert overnight. One of the best ways to improve is to evaluate and critique each use. A third and very important reason for the evaluation step is the message that it sends. Evaluating and discussing the process send the message that the way we interact and communicate with each other is important. This message will go a long way toward enhancing all team work efforts, not just in the area of conflict management.

One final note on Type 3 Conflict: do not ever hesitate to get help with resolving conflict, particularly when you are personally involved. A facilitator who is not part of the conflict and does not have the emotional "ties" to the issue can guide you through the process. Don't feel that just because you are the team leader, you should be able to accomplish everything without assistance. Lean on the facilitator, your sponsor, or any other resources you have available.

Dealing with Difficult Team Members

Every team leader has at least one difficult team member. Handling these members is different than handling conflict. The difficult team member simply has some personality characteristics that cause problems, reduce team effectiveness, or are simply annoying! You can't work through a conflict resolution model because this person generally thinks everyone else is the problem. Rarely does the difficult team member recognize him- or herself as being difficult. So you're asking yourself why this is included in a chapter on conflict. Well, although it is different, it can be as difficult to deal with—and we had to put it somewhere! So read on and see if you can find some answers to help you deal with your difficult team members.

The Constantly Tardy Member

This is the team member who shows up late to almost every meeting—making a commotion, interrupting the flow, asking to be updated. This person can be very annoying to other team members and can sometimes cause others to begin showing up late, knowing the disruption is going to occur anyway.

What do you do?
Whatever you do, don't wait for the constantly tardy member before starting your meeting. When this member does show up, try to keep the flow of the meeting going and ask the person to stick around afterward. After the meeting, simply ask the team member why he or she is late for the meetings. Don't lecture—ask and then truly listen. There could be any number of reasons the person is late. Find out what that reason is and then ask what you can do to help the member be on time. You might ask the person to play a critical role for the next meeting or get their input in setting the meeting time.

Everyone's going to be late sometime. One way to keep disruptions to a minimum is to place the flip chart on the opposite side of the room from the door. When someone comes in late, acknowledge them but don't stop to catch them up. If you're using a flip chart, the notes will help them.

A similar problem person is the team member who always leaves the meeting early. Like the constantly tardy member, finding out why is the key to addressing it.

The Wet Blanket

This is the team member who constantly puts down ideas. "That won't work" is this member's favorite phrase. With this member, you're wrong until you prove yourself right. This problem member can put a damper on the entire team.

What do you do?
The best way to cope with this team member is to use good processes. Get the team to agree on a process to be used and then stick to it. For example, if the team has agreed to use nominal group technique, remind all members of the rule that allows only clarifying questions before starting. You may have to prompt the Wet Blanket a time or two, but the message will eventually sink in.

The Monopolizer

This team member talks so much that he or she dominates the group discussion. It sometimes seems impossible to regain control of the meeting once the monopolizer gets the floor. This problem person often causes other team members to tune out—they know that once the monopolizer gets going, it will be a while.

What do you do?
That old kindergarten trick, round robin, helps here. You may have to invoke a time rule as well. As the team leader, you might say something like, "I'd like to get input on the waste issue. In the interest of time, let's each limit our comments to two minutes." Use the timekeeper to give cues to all members, not just the Monopolizer.

The Opinionated Know-It-All

This person may be related to the Monopolizer. Like the Monopolizer, Know-It-Alls are hard to shut down. However, this team member uses credentials, length of service, age, or some other status to run over others. This difficult person also causes team members' eyes to glaze over, as they lapse into a comatose state.

What do you do?
The number one rule with the Know-It-All is to never challenge his or her expertise. Instead, acknowledge the experience and knowledge, while emphasizing the reason the team has been formed. You might say something like, "There's a very good chance that we'll end up with your original idea, but as a team, we're obligated to consider all options."

The Silent Sam

This team member often sits in the back of the room, doesn't say anything, and frequently ends up with pages and pages of doodles by the end of the meeting. It's hard to get input from the Silent Sam even with a direct question—this person just doesn't have anything to say.

What do you do?
First and foremost, remember your open-ended questions. This is the place to use them. The Silent Sam will give you exactly what you ask for. Call on the Silent Sam specifically when you know that he or she is knowledgeable about the topic. If you don't get an answer right away, let this quiet person off the hook temporarily by saying something like, "Sam, let me give you a chance to think about it. Brenda, how about you?" Then follow up—go back to Silent Sam after Brenda has spoken.

Try this for several meetings before giving up. If your Silent Sam still won't speak up, you may have to meet with him or her away from the meeting and find out what's going on. Try to find a topic that "Sam" would feel comfortable leading a discussion on and put it on the next agenda. The first time you do this, make sure it's only one small part of the meeting so that this difficult team member doesn't feel overwhelmed.

The Side Conversationalist

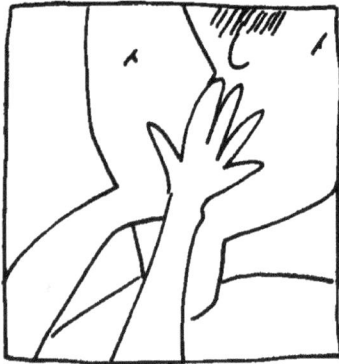

The Side Conversationalist is constantly whispering, gesturing, or writing notes to a neighbor. This problem team member is one of the most difficult to deal with and can be very distracting to the other members.

What do you do?
Try a subtle technique first—if it's the same two people who are always having side conversations, try to sit between them or get someone else to. If your Side Conversationalist can talk to anyone, sit next to him or her yourself. You might also try using the Side Conversationalist as the recorder—it's hard to talk to someone when you're at the flip chart.

If the side conversations continue, you have to confront the Side Conversationalist at a break or after the meeting. Let the Side Conversationalist know that you need his or her input in the meeting and that the side conversations are distracting for you and the other team members.

The Interrupter

This team member is usually well-meaning. The interrupter wants to participate and feels that he or she has something important to add to the discussion. The problem is that this difficult member often starts before someone has finished. He or she blurts out ideas or input regardless of whose turn it is.

What do you do?
Even though this person doesn't mean to be disruptive, the interruptions can cause real problems. The team is looking to you to protect everyone's right for input. You must deal with the Interrupter immediately. You have to jump in with something like, "Wait, let Jean finish her thought." Or remind the Interrupter of the order of the round robin. After the meeting, talk to the Interrupter. You might suggest that he or she bring a pad of paper to jot down thoughts so that they won't be forgotten. Show some empathy; let the person know it's often difficult for you to hold your thought. You might also try using the Interrupter in the recorder role. Recording is a good exercise for improving listening skills.

The Zapper

There are really two types of Zappers—the verbal and the nonverbal. The verbal Zapper's favorite words are "Yeah, right!" The verbal Zapper is generally sarcastic, letting everyone know exactly what he or she thinks of the idea without coming right out and attacking. The nonverbal Zapper can be even worse. This person rolls eyes, shakes the head, slams down books, or furiously writes down notes after something is said. These nonverbals get the message across loud and clear but make it very difficult to confront those messages openly.

What do you do?
Confront the Zapper! Often the Zapper will hide under the guise of humor and say he or she was just kidding around. Push it a little—let the Zapper know that you want to consider all aspects of any option, both good and bad, and that he or she seems to have some ideas/opinions on this one. You might say something like, "Charlie, that comment sounded somewhat sarcastic to me. Is there something about this issue that is bothering you?"

Do the same with the nonverbal Zapper. Bring it out in the open. Say something like, "Jane, something tells me that you're not completely comfortable with this idea. What do you think we should do?" The important thing with the Zapper is to give permission to express feelings but force the input into the open where it can be dealt with. The PIN technique can be helpful if you have a Zapper in your group.

You've read our tips for dealing with difficult team members. However, many of the strategies that we've covered in earlier chapters may also help. The exercise on the following page will test your memory of what you've learned.

Exercise

For each of the difficult team members listed below, write down some tools, processes, or techniques that might help manage the problem behaviors.

Difficult Type	Tools, Processes, or Techniques
The Constantly Tardy Member	
The Wet Blanket	
The Monopolizer	
The Opinionated Know-It-All	
The Silent Sam	
The Side Conversationalist	
The Interrupter	
The Zapper	

See page 24 of the Appendix to compare your answers to the suggested answers.

Additional Conflict Tips

There are a couple of things that you can do to avoid unnecessary conflicts. Every once in a while (every two to three months), the team should go through an exercise to identify the things going well, along with the things not going well. To carry out this exercise, the team brainstorms a list for each of those topics. Once the lists are developed, the team examines the "going well" list and discusses ways to keep up the good work. The team then examines the "not going well" list and develops action steps to address those issues. Like always, those action steps are written down and followed up.

Another tip for reducing the possibility of conflicts is to use team member self-evaluations. These forms are different from the meeting evaluation form we talked about in Chapter 2. The self-evaluation form forces members to examine their own behaviors in the area of teamwork and, hopefully, initiate their own improvements. You can find a copy of the self-evaluation form on page 25 of the Appendix.

One last tip for dealing with conflict—use some mechanism for feedback to other members. Sometimes you have members who are difficult or cause conflict and don't even realize it. If these difficult members are going to improve, they need specific feedback from others. Check with your facilitator or the human resource department to see if there are team member performance appraisals for team members to complete on each other. These appraisals will give team members feedback from all their peers rather than just the team leader or supervisor.

CHAPTER 5

You've made it! You have gone over all the checklists, completed all the steps to get started on the right foot, and you're keeping the team on track and within their boundaries. Now that you have it down pat, it's time to let go of it! All good things come to an end. And hopefully you will be able to look at this team leader experience as a good thing, even though it was probably one of the most challenging assignments you've had.

Disbanding Temporary Teams

Ad hoc teams obviously come to an end—after all, they are temporary teams. Let's start by talking about how to close out an ad hoc team. Once the ad hoc team has completed the project, the sponsor should formally disband the team. Every once in a while a sponsor will forget about this critical step. If that happens, go to the sponsor and discuss it. He or she may have some minor details for the team to address before disbanding. Find out exactly what the team needs to do to complete the project and then get the team focused on tying up those loose ends. The one thing you don't want is for the team to fizzle out with no formal ending. If that happens, it is difficult for team members to look back on the project as a success. No matter how successful the actual project was, the ending will overshadow it.

One of the team's last meetings before officially disbanding should focus on implementation. There are a few important questions to be answered at this final meeting:

If the team has made a change in procedure, are the measures in place to evaluate the change long term?

If the team has made a recommendation, are the key points for successful implementation included?

If the team has made a change in practice or method, is there a plan to publicize the results or "spread the word"?

If you can't answer yes to the questions that apply, the team still has some work to do. It's better to delay disbanding and address all the final details than to have all the work turn out to be for nothing.

Celebrate the Success

Once you have the sponsor's official word on disbanding the team, schedule a formal meeting. Have some kind of ceremony to mark the ending—don't worry about being corny or silly. Buy a couple of bottles of sparkling grape juice and have an official toast to the team's success. Find ways to recognize each team member's contribution to the team. Give some high-fives and pat members' backs. It is important that members leave with the knowledge that each person's participation was appreciated and important.

Standing and natural teams do not have an ending to the team, but they often rotate leadership. There are some things you can do as the current team leader to make this rotation go smoothly.

Record Keeping

The team leader may be charged with the responsibility of keeping up with the team's records. One of the best ways to organize these records is with a team logbook. This logbook should include the team charter, the team's ground rules, along with the agendas, action minutes, and parking lot forms from past meetings. On some teams, the scribe has responsibility for keeping the logbook. If that's the case, get the logbook from the scribe so that you and the new team leader can go over it. Carefully review past agendas, showing how the agenda items are written with an action verb. The two of you should work together to develop the agendas for the next few meetings.

Coleading the Team

If it would be helpful, you and the new team leader could colead a couple of meetings to ease the transition. This gives the new leader time to get adjusted to this new role without having to jump in headfirst. It also gives the members an opportunity to become accustomed to the new team leader.

Subteam Leaders

Another tip for sharing leadership on standing and natural teams is to use subteams whenever possible. Often, these permanent teams run into problems and issues. You remember that when that happens, the permanent team sponsors an ad hoc team to solve the problem or deal with the issue. You do not need to be the leader of that subteam—as a matter of fact, this is the perfect opportunity to develop leadership skills in whomever is slated to become the next team leader. Leading the subteam allows him or her to gain some experience as leader on a smaller scale, making the later transition easier.

We're approaching the finish line here. By working your way through this book, you have made sure that the team has all the necessary support elements in place—a named sponsor, a clearly understood charter, and a mission or purpose. After getting started right, you then provided the leadership to keep the team on the right track through meeting-management skills, problem-solving techniques, and conflict-resolution methods. And now, you have made sure that the team has finished with a flourish—by either disbanding with a bang or ensuring a smooth transition from one leader to the next. Now it's time to pat yourself on the back—bask a little bit in some praise for yourself! Leading a team is challenging and sometimes downright hard, but you did it. And hopefully as part of all this continuous improvement—improvement of interaction between team members, improvement in problem solving, improvement in work processes—you also had opportunity for improvement in your own abilities. If you take a minute to look at how you've grown in your analytical ability, in your interpersonal abilities, and in your leadership ability, you just might surprise yourself. On the following page, there is one last exercise in continuous improvement—a self-scoring assessment of your performance as team leader. Take a few minutes to complete the questionnaire and identify what you have done well and what you could continue to improve upon the next time you lead a team.

Exercise

Write a checkmark (✓) in the column that best reflects your behavior.

	Never	Sometimes	Always
Structure			
I ensured that . . . Team members had an opportunity to clarify the charter.			
Members understood the purpose of the team.			
Meeting Management			
I ensured that . . . Agendas were developed with input from others.			
Agendas were distributed in advance of the meeting.			
Roles were appointed at the beginning of meetings.			
Ground rules were reviewed at the beginning of meetings.			
Action items were written down with specific names and time frames assigned.			
Assignments were fairly distributed.			
Parking lot items were followed up.			
Meetings were evaluated and the team followed up on suggestions.			
Participation			
I ensured that . . . All team members had a chance to speak.			
I used open-ended, direct questions.			
I encouraged others to ask clarifying questions.			
All members' opinions or views were protected from attack.			
Team members saw differences of opinion as an opportunity for innovative approaches.			
The team worked toward consensus and didn't fall back on voting.			
I recognized the input of all members.			

	Never	Sometimes	Always
Resources			
I ensured that . . . When the team needed outside resources and support, we asked for it.			
The team sought direction or guidance from the sponsor when needed.			
When our recommendations were turned down, the team received an explanation.			
Problem Solving			
I ensured that . . . The team focused on each phase of the process (problem definition, cause identification, solution analysis).			
I did not fall into the trap of jumping to solutions.			
The team followed up on solutions and evaluated and adjusted as needed.			
The team publicized the results of problem-solving efforts.			
Continuous Improvement			
I ensured that . . . The team constantly looked for ways to improve processes (both work and team processes).			
The team used the critical tools of process improvement.			
Conflict			
I ensured that . . . Conflict was dealt with directly and with respect for all individuals.			
I dealt with difficult team members rather than allowing them to disrupt the team processes.			
I modeled the behavior expected of others when I was involved in a conflict.			
I helped others see their role in creating the conflict and identify what they could do to resolve it.			

APPENDIX

Ad Hoc Team Charter

Goal Statement and Success Criteria: Identify causes of scrap on Line #2 and reduce it by 50%

Team Sponsor: Dan Jones

Team Leader: Bill Little

Assigned Facilitator: Susan Lide

Time Frame: 3 months

Names of Team Members

Gail Williams

Lois Menendez

John Duncan

Will Gordon

Boundaries

- The team cannot change product specifications.
- The team cannot purchase new equipment without department head approval.
- The team can request assistance from engineering for equipment modifications.
- The team can request bids from vendors.

Budget/Resources

- No dollar amount budgeted
- May meet on overtime (1 hour per week)
- Maintenance—Mike Mays
- Engineering—John Latimer

Standing Team Charter

Team Purpose/Mission: The Safety Team's purpose is to create a safe, accident-free workplace.

Team Sponsor: Chuck McClure

Assigned Facilitator: John Adams

Names of Team Members

Nadine Johnson (team leader)

Kent McCall

Judy Morris

Andy Danson

Susan Smith

Boundaries

- May not change existing safety policy without approval from Plant Manager
- May conduct audits in any department
- May require immediate change in safety practices if necessary

Budget/Resources

- $10,000 for Safety Award Program
- Word processing support from Plant Manager's office

Natural Team Charter

Team Name: _B-5 Team—Second Shift_

Team's Purpose: _Produce widgets that meet or exceed quality standards_

Team Job Description: _Team is responsible for preventive maintenance, housekeeping, supplying internal customers, and providing break coverage._

Team Sponsor: _John Lowe_

Assigned Facilitator: _John Jeffers_

Team Members: _Scott Sloan, Glenn Jenkins, Bernie Williams, Lisa Stone_

Decision-Making Authority

- Team may write work orders for routine maintenance and breakdowns.
- Team will determine break schedules and vacation coverage.
- Team will determine weekly meeting.

Boundaries

- Team must notify supervisor if repair will affect production schedule.
- At least two team members must be in work area at all times.
- Team may <u>not</u> meet more than one hour per week.

Answers to Charter Exercises

Ad Hoc Team Charter

This problem statement points to a specific cause—the paper-work. If the team is limited to attacking only that cause of shipping delays, the solution may be less than satisfactory. The problem statement also does not specify the percentage or amount of reduction in complaints expected. A better problem statement might be:

> Reduce customer service complaints due to shipping delays by 50 percent.

This statement is specific but does not point the team toward a particular cause. This will allow the team to analyze all possible causes and ensure that the root cause of the delays is acted on. This statement also tells the team specifically what is expected in the way of outcomes. See sample on page app-1.

Standing Team Charter

This is a very broad purpose for the team. However, that's OK for a standing team. The real problem with this charter is that the boundaries are missing. These team members have no idea of what they can and can't do. If the team members don't know, neither will the rest of the organization. This will certainly impact on the team's effectiveness. Members may react with paralysis—an inability to act on anything. Or they may go overboard, stepping all over everyone with an inflated sense of power. Clear boundaries or empowerment limits need to be added to this charter. See sample on page app-2.

Natural Team Charter

This team has a good, clear purpose statement, along with well-stated responsibilities. There are also specific boundaries. The missing element in this charter is the resources. The sponsor should specify available resources. Resources might include names of people the team can turn to for guidance or support, an overtime budget, or an assigned contact person in shipping. See sample on page app-3.

Training Survey

Please list the courses or seminars you have attended in the past year on the following topics. Please include the approximate date of attendance.

Team Building/Interpersonal Skills

_____

_____

_____

Problem-Solving/Statistical Process Control/Data Analysis Techniques

_____

_____

_____

Meeting Participation/Meeting Management Skills

_____

_____

_____

Conflict Resolution/Conflict Management

_____

_____

_____

TEAM MISSION STATEMENT—Example

Who we are and what we do:

The B-52 team exists to

- produce the highest quality widgets as efficiently as possible;

- solve problems in our process quickly and effectively, with input from all team members; and

- always look for better and more efficient ways of producing our widgets.

We will accomplish these goals by valuing one another's opinions, treating one another with respect, and developing a supportive work environment.

Signatures of Team Members:

_____   _____

_____   _____

_____   _____

Writing Your Mission Statement— Worksheet

Mission statements are important because they state the direction your team is supposed to head. They serve as a lantern, guiding your tasks and activities as a team.

What is the purpose of your team?

    As a team, your mission is most likely to produce a product, to perform an operation on an existing product, or to offer a service to some internal or external customer.

Write down three to five reasons why your team exists. What is your team supposed to accomplish or be responsible for? Who is your customer?

_____

_____

_____

_____

Write down some words that describe the quality you are striving for in your product/service.

_____

_____

_____

_____

Write down some words that describe how you want your team to behave toward one another.

_____

_____

_____

_____

Measurement Planning Table—Example

Team Name: _Line #5 Team_   **Team Sponsor:** _Donna Donnelly_

Goal: _Reduce the scrap produced on Line #5 by 50 percent by January 1._

	Measurement 1	Measurement 2	Measurement 3	Measurement 4
What will be measured?	Percent of scrap			
How will it be measured?	Scrap will be weighed and recorded every 4 hours			
Team member responsible for measurement	utility operator			
How long will it be measured?	1 month			
What will be considered a successful solution?	50 percent reduction			

Measurement Planning Table

Team Name: _____   Team Sponsor: _____

Goal: _____

	Measurement 1	Measurement 2	Measurement 3	Measurement 4
What will be measured?				
How will it be measured?				
Team member responsible for measurement				
How long will it be measured?				
What will be considered a successful solution?				

Meeting Roles
Rotation Roster

Meeting Role	Who Is Responsible	Date
Leader		
Timekeeper		
Gatekeeper		
Recorder		
Judge		
Devil's Advocate		
Coach		
Scribe		
Other		

Parking Lot

Note: One of three things must happen: (1) items need to be resolved or (2) placed on this parking lot or (3) assigned to someone as an action step.

Item #	Remarks
1	
2	
3	
4	
5	
6	

Action Minutes

Note: One of three things must happen: (1) items need to be resolved or (2) placed on the parking lot or (3) entered on this action plan.

Action Item	Assigned to	Target Date for Completion	Status
Call vendors for quotes on new threading apparatus			
Work with Jim in Engineering to schedule machine modifications during holiday break			
Get list of operators willing to work overtime week of 12-28			

Answers to Involvement Exercise

Case #1

One of your team members always sits off to the side of the room—not joining others at the table. When you try to get him to join the others, he always says he's more comfortable where he is. What should you do?

Set the room up ahead of time so that all chairs are situated around the table. If he moves the chair away from the table when he comes in, ask him to remain at the table so that he can participate more fully in the meeting. If the team member persists in staying on the outskirts of the meeting, meet with him one-on-one to try to find out why.

Case #2

Your team members always wander in late. Meetings almost always start 10 to 15 minutes late because even when team members get there, they want to socialize for a minute or two. What should you do?

Schedule some time (about 5 minutes) at the beginning of the meeting for "catch up." This will allow team members to get greetings and small talk out of the way. Then start the meeting at the scheduled time, regardless of who is there. Get team members accustomed to the fact that meetings are going to start on time. You may want to lead a brief discussion on the best start time for meetings. Once you all agree on a time, get verbal commitment from the members to show up on time.

Case #3

One team member always starts every discussion, always has a comment or observation after someone else speaks, and always tries to have the last word. What technique(s) can you use to deal with this team member?

Use round robin for all discussions. Revisit the ground rules and, if needed, add a ground rule about speaking out of turn. Appoint a strong judge who reminds all members of the ground rule and the round robin.

Case #4

Your team does a good job of meeting management. It holds good discussions and usually reaches agreement on decisions. However, there is very little follow through on decisions. Many of the good ideas have never been implemented. How should you address this?

Use the action minutes form and ensure that assignments have a target date. Review the action form at each meeting and ask the team member with responsibility for the assignment to update the team on the status. If there is an assignment that continues to be incomplete, determine whether the team members need additional resources to complete the assignment.

Case #5

You have one team member who never speaks up. Even when you use round robin, this member passes when a turn comes around. What else can you try?

Meet with this team member and help him or her prepare for the next meeting. Find an area that this member feels comfortable with and help him or her prepare for the discussion. Generally, quiet members will participate more if they know when you are going to call on them and have a chance to prepare ahead of time.

Case #6

Your team members have good discussions, but they never stick to the agenda. Often they get off on a completely different topic for the entire meeting, never making it back to the original agenda item. Since the team is dealing with work-related topics, should you do anything at all? Why or why not?

Yes, you should definitely address this issue. The agenda allows team members to prepare, and it helps keep the group focused on the right goals. If the team is straying from the agenda, perhaps the agenda itself is a problem. Involve the others in setting the agenda, either by doing it at the end of each meeting, or by posting it where everyone has access. Also, appoint a strong gatekeeper to keep the group on track. If the team is effective without sticking to an agenda, just think what kind of results you can expect when they become focused.

Team Meeting Evaluation

Circle your response to the following questions.

	Very Little	Little	Some	Quite a Bit
1. To what extent did others pay attention to your input?	1	2	3	4
2. Did the team use consensus to make team decisions?	1	2	3	4
3. To what extent did you actively seek contributions from others on the team?	1	2	3	4
4. How responsible and committed do you feel for the decisions that were made?	1	2	3	4

5. What should the team do next time to improve its performance?

_____

_____

_____

_____

_____

_____

_____

Problem Solving/ Continuous Improvement Resources

The Memory Jogger Plus+
Michael Brassard
Goal/QPC 1989
508-685-3900

The Team Handbook
Peter S. Scholtes
Joiner Associates
800-669-8326

SPC Simplified—Practical Steps to Quality
Robert T. Amsden, Howard E. Butler,
Davida M. Amsden
UNIPUB/Kraus Int. Publications
One Water Street
White Plains, NY 10601

In Search of Solutions—60 Ways to
Guide Your Problem-Solving Group
David Quinlivan-Hall, David Renner
Phieffer & Company

The Deming Route to
Quality and Productivity—
Roadmaps and Roadblocks
William W. Scherkenbach
Mercury Press, Rockville, MD
301-770-6177

The Deming Management Method
Mary Walton
The Putnam Publishing Group
200 Madison Avenue, NY, NY 10016

Quality is Free—The Art of
Making Quality Certain
Phillip Crosby
Penguin Books USA Inc.
375 Hudson Street, NY, NY 10014

The Memory Jogger—
A Pocket Guide for
Continuous Improvement
Goal/QPC 1998
508-685-3900

The Problem-Solving Toolbox
Cornelius & Associates
Products and Services for Teams
800-200-1104

How to Construct a Checksheet

Instructions

Step 1: Determine all items within a process or system that need to be monitored.

Step 2: Categorize all pertinent data that should be viewed together.

Step 3: Develop a grid or matrix that lists each item.

Step 4: Determine a specific time frame to measure and include in the matrix.

Step 5: Record data based on the design of the matrix.

Step 6: Examine data at intervals that will provide the most benefit for each particular application.

Example

Reasons for Service Delays
Month of January

	Week 1	Week 2	Week 3	Week 4		Total
New Personnel	✔✔✔	✔✔	✔	✔✔	→	8
New Procedure	✔✔	✔✔	✔	✔	→	6
Equipment Failure	✔✔✔✔	✔✔✔	✔✔✔✔✔	✔✔✔	→	15
Lack of Personnel	✔	—	✔✔	✔	→	4
Lack of Supplies	✔✔	✔✔✔	✔✔✔	✔✔	→	10
Total	12	10	12	9		

Answers to Problem-Solving Exercise

Statement #1
Waste is sky-high! We have to get it under control.

Waste on the extrusion line is at 21.25 percent. It should be no higher than 10 percent.

Statement #2
We must do something about team members who take too many breaks and stay too long.

We are entitled to two 20 minute breaks each day. Some team members are taking three breaks and not coming within 20 minutes.

Statement #3
We've got to improve quality—we had 15,000 yards of rejected fabric last month!

The number of yards of rejected fabric for the month of March was 15,000. The team goal is to have less than 2,500 yards of rejected fabric per month.

Statement #4
Housekeeping is terrible—if we don't get this place cleaned up, someone will get hurt.

Our housekeeping standard requires tools to be kept in the tool bin when not in use and the work area to be swept twice during the shift. Our tools are frequently left out on machines and our area is only being swept at the end of the shift.

Answers to Cost-Benefit Exercise

Costs

$ 7,500
$ 2,200
$ 1,500
$ 750
$ 1,200
―――――
$13,150   Total Costs

Benefits

$75,000—$150,000 divided by 2 (50 percent savings)
$ 5,000—$25,000 × .20 (20 percent decrease in
                         billing errors)
$80,000—savings per year

Savings for first year	=	$ 66,850	(80,000 − 13,150)
Savings for years 2–5	=	$320,000	(80,000 × 4)
Total savings over 5 years	=	$386,850	

Answers to Conflict Exercise— Opening a Resolution Session

1. You are the leader of a natural team with two team members who are always talking to other team members about the other one. Each one believes that the other one does not do his/her share of the work, both on the work floor and in team assignments. However, they won't talk to each other about it. How should you open your conflict resolution session?

   John, Bob, I'd like to discuss the relationship between you two. You each seem to have problems with the other's work habits and follow-through on assignments. However, you don't seem to be able to talk through it with each other. I'd like for the three of us to try to work this out.

2. You are the leader of a project team. The team has a very short time frame. There are two members who are always blocking decisions. You use nominal group technique to narrow down options, but these two members always seem to get stuck on two ideas and neither one will back down. They often take up most of the team meeting debating about the option each one supports. How should you open your conflict resolution session?

   I feel that our team is having real problems with reaching consensus and that it may be due to the frequent discussions you two have about your preferred options. Sometimes those discussions turn into a debate involving only you two. I'd like for us to find a way to break out of this cycle—can we talk about that in this meeting today?

3. You are the team leader of a standing team that has just changed membership due to rotation. One member of the original team has already developed a strong dislike for one of the new members. They often interrupt each other during team meetings and try to talk over each other. Your facilitator does a good job of enforcing the ground rules and usually gets them to stop, but then they each seem to sit back and "check out" for the remainder of the meeting. How should you open your conflict resolution session?

I have noticed during our meetings that each of you sometimes interrupts the other or tries to interject during the other person's turn at round robin. When our judge enforces the "no interruptions" ground rule, you both seem to stop participating for the rest of the meeting. I would like to try to see if we can work out a solution that will keep both of you active in our meetings—we need your input.

Answers to Conflict Exercise— Giving Your Views

"When you come on so strong in the team meeting, everybody else just shuts down. You don't seem to think that anybody else has anything useful to say."

When you talk out of turn during the round robin and interrupt others, some team members don't feel as if their input is valued and simply stop contributing.

"You're always late to every single meeting we have. You don't have any consideration for other team members' time."

When you come into the team meeting after we have started, it is very distracting for other team members.

"I don't think you care if this team succeeds in solving our problem. No matter what I do to try to get you to take responsibility for your action items, you never follow up."

When you don't follow through on your assigned action item, the team has trouble meeting project deadlines.

"When you constantly ignore the ground rules of the team, other members feel like they can break them too. We've got to work on this!"

When you use profanity (or any other specific ground rule) despite our ground rule against it, it gives others the impression that the ground rules are not serious.

Answers to Difficult Team Member Exercise

Difficult Type	Tools, Processes, or Techniques
The Constantly Tardy Member	Ground rules, judge, ask for input on setting the meeting time
The Wet Blanket	PIN, rules of brainstorming
The Monopolizer	Ground rules, judge, limit on round robin
The Opinionated Know-It-All	Nominal group technique, 10-4
The Silent Sam	Round robin, asking the Silent Sam to develop an agenda item and lead the discussion for that portion of the meeting
The Side Conversationalist	Ground rules, judge, assigning the Side Conversationalist to be the recorder
The Interrupter	Ground rules, judge, round robin
The Zapper	Ground rules, judge, PIN

My Contribution to the Team— A Self-Evaluation

Write a checkmark (✓) in the column that best reflects your behavior.

Action	Most of the Time	Some of the Time	Not at All
I volunteer for meeting roles.			
I come to the meetings prepared.			
I complete all my action items assigned at meetings.			
I give ideas, suggestions, and input.			
I listen carefully and attentively to the input, ideas, and suggestions of others.			
I express differing or opposing views with tact and respect for the other person.			
I make efforts to keep the group on track.			
I explain my ideas with examples or illustrations.			
I ask others for their views or ideas.			
I refrain from interrupting when others are speaking.			
I summarize what I hear others saying.			
I actively encourage quiet members.			
I try to help find areas of agreement when there are conflicting points of view.			
When we are trying to reach consensus, I look for the best decision rather than arguing for my preference.			
I test for consensus.			
I avoid side-conversations.			
I volunteer for action items.			
I give input on the planning of the next meeting.			